Bernedoodles: A Head To Tail Guide

Sherry Rupke

with Sandy Rideout

24

Foreword

I have the best job in the world. It's not the easiest job, or the most glamorous. I usually start my day cleaning up after the dogs, and most days end that way, too. I am constantly on the go delivering pups to the airport for shipping, buying hundreds of pounds of food, taking blood samples and dropping them at the lab, breeding dogs, handling puppies, and bottle-feeding on a strict schedule. Then, often in the middle of the night, a dog will go into labour and I'll step in as midwife.

Running the business fills the cracks of my day. There are hundreds of e-mails from prospective and current owners to answer. Arrangements to make and problems to solve. Research to do on breeding stock. Puppy photos to take and post on my website. Applications to review. Temperament testing to do. Matching of puppies with new owners. Exploring the myriad issues related to building a new kennel and resort.

It's pretty much non-stop, even with several staff. But all of this work eventually builds to the one glorious moment that makes everything worthwhile: placing a puppy into the arms of its new owners and seeing their faces light up with joy.

I realize how lucky I am to spend my life bringing people and dogs together. If ever I have doubts—say, after missing another family event because of the dogs—all I need to do is check my e-mail inbox. It is full of notes from people saying my dogs have made a huge difference in their lives.

On top of that, I get to use my training, skills, and hard-won knowledge to develop strong breeding lines. I've chosen to focus all my energy on hybrids, because, when bred correctly, the dogs are generally much healthier than their purebred parents. This is particularly true of the Bernedoodle—a cross between the Bernese Mountain Dog and the Poodle.

I began breeding purebred Bernese Mountain Dogs in 1998. I love the "Berner" for its beauty and sweet nature, but it is a tragically short-lived dog. People have told me heartbreaking stories about losing their beloved Berner as early as age four or five to cancer. Others lamented their dog's painful muscular-skeletal problems, such as hip dysplasia. I wanted to help them—to produce a healthier Berner—but no matter how carefully a breeder selects her lines, there is only so much you can do to counter a hundred years of inbreeding.

Instead, I chose to branch out. I wanted to see if I could retain the character and appearance of the Berner while gaining health advantages through hybrid vigor. The Poodle was an obvious candidate for the mix, having brought so much to other hybrids. In fact, I was already seeing success with the Goldendoodle and producing stable dogs that showed far fewer health problems than their purebred ancestors. They were becoming extremely popular and beloved family pets.

I put a great deal of care into developing my Goldendoodle lines, and when I began dabbling with Bernedoodles, I assumed there would be a lot of crossover. But the Bernedoodle has proven to be a greater challenge—and not just in achieving the coveted tri-colour coat. At first, I worked on this hybrid on the side, a litter here, a litter there, watching the results, listening to my clients. When people started raving about the Bernedoodle's sweet, loving nature, I knew I had a winner on my hands.

Despite starting my career as a breeder of purebreds, my only goal has been to produce loveable, fun, stable, healthy puppies that fit into any family. All my dogs are beautiful, but they are not show dogs, nor are they bred to be. They are meant to be at your side no matter whether you are hiking, snowshoeing, or lying on the couch watching a movie. Their only job is to be your best friend. The Bernedoodle is designed expressly for that purpose. It blends the clever goofiness of the poodle with the placid loyalty of the Bernese. What's more, the Bernedoodle is low- to non-shedding, and is a safe bet for most people with allergies.

To me, the Bernedoodle is a perfect companion dog. I must qualify that by saying that it's important to find the perfect Bernedoodle *for you*. As with any hybrid, there can be considerable variation within and across litters. The size, coat type, temperament and energy level may differ significantly among siblings. While it is always important to buy a puppy from a professional breeder, in the case of a hybrid like the Bernedoodle, it's even more critical to have an expert's help. Breeders who have spent years watching dogs develop can usually predict with reasonable accuracy how a hybrid puppy is likely to turn out. Without that professional guidance, you will get surprises—not all of them welcome.

What I deliver is a pup from stable, healthy parents that has the potential to be *your* perfect dog. After that, it's mostly up to you. Careful training and socialization bring that promise to fruition.

In this book, I will share much of what I know about Bernedoodles. I never have enough time to spend with new owners when they pick up their puppies. Further, many of my pups are shipped to far flung destinations. Although I send a package of information home with every pup, if you want to raise a puppy to be a respectful and dedicated companion, there is much more to learn. This book will allow me to provide detail on hybrids in general, the Bernedoodle in particular, and will cover the basics of raising a good canine citizen.

The SwissRidge "community" has grown significantly in recent years, and I have a very special relationship with the owners of my puppies, supported by social media. When I decided to write this book, I didn't have far to go to find ideas about what to cover. Much of the information I've included here comes at the request of my clients, who kindly completed surveys and shared their comments about Bernedoodles. Many people stepped forward with stories, questions, testimonials, and photos.

This book is meant to be a primer on Bernedoodles—to gather in one place the key information I provide to clients. Many of the questions I receive relate to training, so I've included a section from my partner, trainer Lucas Mucha. Lucas works wonders with all manner of dogs, and has developed special insight into Bernedoodles and Goldendoodles from working with my clients and their pets.

The breed is still young, and as more information becomes available, I will add to this body of knowledge. Please continue to share your insights with me, and join the SwissRidge Kennel Facebook group. I also update my website regularly at http://www.swissridgekennels.com/

All photos in this book are of dogs from SwissRidge Kennels. It was very hard to choose from so many beautiful photos of my clients' dogs. I hereby commit to posting more on my website. Guaranteed to make you smile!

Chapter 1

Introducing the Bernedoodle

The Bernedoodle is, quite simply, a cross between a Bernese Mountain Dog and a Poodle. I coined the name, "Bernedoodle," when I began breeding them in 2003. To my knowledge, I was the first person to begin deliberately breeding these dogs, although it's entirely possible a few casual (or accidental) crosses occurred before that.

My guess is that few breeders saw the great potential in this match. And to be honest, I didn't initially see it myself. I had been breeding Bernese Mountain Dogs for years, as well as Golden Retrievers, but most of my time and effort went into my Goldendoodles—a Golden Retriever and Poodle cross. It was my clients that suggested pairing one of my Berners with my purebred Standard Poodle. Curious by nature, I decided to give it a try.

I was pleased with the results, but I could see that developing a great Bernedoodle line would be more challenging than I'd expected, and I still had my hands full with my Goldendoodles. Although I produced a few litters of Bernedoodles here and there, I largely kept that project on the back burner for years.

Word nonetheless began to get out about the Bernedoodle and as interest grew, I started paying more attention. I became more deliberate in my pairings, trying to figure out how to get the result I wanted. Then, when I began producing tri-color pups more consistently in 2011, these dogs became something of an overnight sensation.

While the Bernedoodle's popularity is growing, the breed is still relatively rare. If you own one, you are likely to be questioned often about your dog's origins. Many of them are striking, with a cuddly, panda bear quality that attracts people like a magnet.

An owner says… *Prepare to get stopped constantly. It is hard to take a walk on a busy street without being stopped every few minutes by people in awe at his cuteness and wanting to know what in the world this breed is!*

But good looks are only part of the Bernedoodle's appeal. They've got the whole package.

An owner says… *The Bernedoodle has surpassed my expectations. They are everything I want, plus a lot more. They have tons of personality. They're happy hiking, and they're happy hanging out and being lazy. They are easy to train, and they enjoy learning. They hold my gaze longer than any other dog I've had. They are individuals.*

The Bernese Mountain Dog

My long history with Bernese Mountain Dogs has given me a deep appreciation for their placid, easygoing nature and extreme loyalty. In general, "Berners" tend to prefer the company of people to dogs, and they are completely dedicated to their families, with a special fondness for children. In fact, they are so loyal that it can be difficult to re-home an adult Berner and break its original bond. Berners are known for leaning on people to soak up all possible attention.

It goes without saying that Berners are exceptionally beautiful dogs with their distinctive tri-colored coats. The breed standard features a shiny black coat, with rust colored markings above the eyes, at the sides of the mouth, on the legs, and a small amount around the chest. The perfectly marked Berner also has a white muzzle, a white blaze on its head, four white paws, a white cross on the chest and a white tail tip.

Bred in the Swiss Alps as farm dogs that pulled carts or drove cattle to market, the Bernese thrives in cold weather, and has a double coat that sheds quite heavily. It's an intelligent, strong dog that has a moderate need for exercise. This versatile breed does well in agility, tracking, herding, and therapy work.

Despite their affectionate nature and gorgeous looks, however, the Bernese Mountain Dog nearly became extinct in the late 1800s. The effort to bring them back led to inbreeding that has increased the incidence of serious health problems. A significant number of Bernese are afflicted with hip and elbow dysplasia, or succumb to inherited cancer, heart disease, or epilepsy in middle age.

> **An owner says…** *We love Bernese Mountain Dogs. We have had two who had very short lives. We are hoping that with a mixed breed our dog will be healthier than our Bernese were.*

While cancer is the leading cause of death for dogs in general, Bernese Mountain Dogs have a much higher rate of fatal cancer than other breeds. Purebred Bernese are frequently stricken with malignant histiocytosis, a genetic cancer of the lungs and lymph nodes.

Overall, the Berner is one of the shorter-lived dog breeds, with a life expectancy of just seven years. This is particularly sad when the Berner is known to be slow to mature, and somewhat challenging to train. Owners may enjoy only a short period of blissful companionship with a well-behaved dog before it begins a decline into sickness and old age.

> **An owner says…** *I had bad luck with the health of my Bernese Mountain Dogs, and turned to the Bernedoodle because mixed breed dogs are likely to have fewer health issues. In addition, I wanted a dog that would love the water and enjoy swimming—a trait that is not common in the Bernese but is common in Poodles.*

Inbreeding has also had an impact on the Berner's temperament. Without proper socialization, these naturally cautious and reserved dogs can become skittish and suspicious, and may develop separation anxiety. They can also be decidedly stubborn.

Yet the Bernese Mountain Dog also has a deep need to please its humans and is surprisingly sensitive. As a result, training a Berner requires a great deal of patience and a gentle hand.

The Poodle

Everyone knows that the Poodle ranks high on the canine intelligence scale. They are very trainable and excel in obedience. Most people are also aware that their low- to non-shedding coat makes poodles a great choice for those with allergies. What many *don't* realize, however, is how goofy and fun poodles are. They are the clowns of the doggie world, and it's no coincidence they were used in circus acts for centuries.

But the Poodle is more than a clever show dog: it is believed to have originated as a water retriever, in Germany. This breed doesn't get nearly enough credit for being a hardy, intrepid dog that enjoys outdoor adventures.

Poodles come in three sizes and a wide variety of colors, including white, black, blue, gray, silver, brown, apricot, and red. There are also "parti" color Poodles, which have a white base and patches of another solid color, or "phantom" Poodles, which have a base of one color complemented with points of another.

Where most dogs have double coats, poodles have a single layer coat of dense, curly fur that sheds minimally but does mat without proper care.

A typical Poodle is lively and playful, with a bouncy prance to its walk. It thrives best in a busy household where it can get plenty of attention and stimulation. Vigorous exercise and ongoing training are the keys to managing the Poodle's exuberance. If bored, Poodles may get into mischief. They are also quick to sound an alert, and have earned a reputation for barking.

Inbreeding is common in Poodles, as well. That has led to some Poodles being high strung and sensitive to stress. Further, it's led to serious health problems, including eye, skin, and digestive diseases, as well as immune system diseases. The most common problems are bloat/torsion, thyroid issues, tracheal collapse, epilepsy, sebaceous adenitis, juvenile renal disease, hip dysplasia, and cancer. Standard poodles tend to have a lifespan of about 11-12 years, with miniature and toy poodles living longer.

The Glory of the Hybrid

Some people deride the current trend in cross-breeding "designer dogs" as a marketing ploy, but the health advantages have been proven.

If a breeder does his or her due diligence in selecting the right parents, crossing purebred dogs of different breeds results in puppies that are healthier than either of their parents. This is because the two breeds are generally prone to different genetic problems. Hybrids such as the Bernedoodle are only likely to inherit a health problem that is common to both the Poodle *and* the Bernese—two breeds that share few common diseases. Bernedoodles therefore have what is referred to as "hybrid vigor," and can be expected to live healthier, longer lives than their purebred parents.

A hybrid dog combines the traits and characteristics of its purebred parents; with careful, conscientious breeding, the resulting pups may end up with the best attributes of each. In the case of the Bernedoodle, the blend of the Bernese Mountain Dog and the Poodle produces a smart, friendly, playful dog. They tend to have the sweetness and loyalty of the Bernese, and the goofy liveliness of the Poodle. Like the Bernese, they are gentle around children and the elderly, and because they love to work, they often make excellent therapy dogs. This is appealing to many owners:

> *"I take her to visit in my mother's retirement home and she just seems to sense that she needs to settle and be gentle in that setting."*

> *"He is very intuitive and gentle natured especially with elderly people or young kids. He is never too rough with them."*

Most Bernedoodles have a moderate activity level. They love to play, run, and hike with you, and may inherit the Poodle's love for retrieving and swimming. When it's time to relax, Bernedoodles are usually happy to join you on the couch—on your lap, if you let them. Most of them have little need for personal space.

In my survey of owners, people commonly used the following words to describe their Bernedoodles: charming, curious, friendly, social, enthusiastic, cuddly, and loving. The three words that came up in nearly *every* survey were "happy," "smart," and "goofy."

All of these words make a breeder's heart sing!

A Slight Exaggeration

An owner says... *He is perfect. Exactly what we'd hoped for.*

Are Bernedoodles perfect? Of course not. While many owners I surveyed used the word "perfect," another word also appeared frequently: "stubborn." Also, there were several variations on the word "energetic." Granted, many of these dogs are still young, and will mellow out considerably as they mature. Still, when a word like "stubborn" comes up that often, it needs to be acknowledged. The Bernese Mountain Dog is notorious for its stubbornness, so it's to be expected that the trait would appear in the hybrid, too.

Lastly, Bernedoodles may also inherit the Berner's sensitivity. What this means is that Bernedoodles not only need to be taught right from wrong, their training also requires patience, a light touch, and positive reinforcement.

An owner says: She is also very 'soft.' She doesn't like to have someone raise their voice at her and really needs to be treated kindly.

Unless a breeder is vigilant, Bernedoodles may also inherit the Berner's cautiousness with strangers and end up being somewhat skittish. Further, from the Poodle, they can inherit an extremely high level of energy. Conscientious breeders need to work hard to avoid these traits by being very selective in the dogs they breed.

When bred well, however, I agree with my clients that the Bernedoodle is an intelligent, social, fun, crossbreed with character and charisma. On the whole, Bernedoodles tend to be quite similar to Goldendoodles in nature, with the most notable difference being that the Bernedoodle can be headstrong. This is more pronounced at the puppy stage, and tends to disappear when the Bernedoodle is older and trained. Every dog has a different personality, but the two breeds have much in common, and those traits make them excellent family pets.

I am also working very hard, via selective breeding, to reduce or eliminate stubbornness in the Bernedoodle. Feedback from my clients suggests I'm well on the way to reaching this goal.

The Fairest of Them All

Did you know that… the curlier the dog's coat, the better it is for people with allergies?

The Bernedoodle is an attractive dog—in some cases, a traffic-stopping dog. They tend to be pure black, black-and-white, black-and-brown, or tri-colour (black, white and brown), but I have seen other colors. Depending on the color pattern, the bi-colors can be quite striking, and the tri-colors are drop-dead gorgeous.

Their overall appearance combines elements of the Bernese and the Poodle. Chapter 4 will explore the range in size, shape, and temperament within a single litter of Bernedoodles. Suffice it to say at this point that, beyond color, well chosen parents tend to blend the traits of the Poodle and the Berner in a fairly consistent way. Although some pups may lean more toward the Poodle's slighter build, or the Berner's sheer bulk, there is a common "look," and a breeder can, to some extent, control that by studying the results of matching various pairs.

Many, if not most, of my clients want a tri-color Bernedoodle, with markings as similar as possible to those of the Bernese Mountain Dog. That look is extremely challenging to achieve, and a work-in-progress to be explored further in Chapter 3.

While I, too, appreciate the beauty of the typical Bernese markings, I love Bernedoodles of all colors. After all, I am a breeder of hybrids, which by very definition means I value uniqueness.

Sneeze-proofing a Dog

Every Bernedoodle has a different coat. My personal preference is a coat with soft, loose, flowing waves that is easy to groom but generally low- to non-shedding.

The majority of Bernedoodles have a wavy coat that sheds minimally, if at all. You may see a bit of fur in your brush and the occasional "dust bunny." Most people with allergies to dog dander (i.e., those who experience sneezing and runny eyes) are fine with a wavy-coated dog.

In my experience, it's rare to see a Bernedoodle with a straight coat. However, the straighter the coat, the more it sheds, and the less suitable the dog will be for people with allergies.

> **Did you know that...** the longer your dog's coat grows, the straighter it becomes? Even a curly-haired dog's coat may look wavy when kept long, as the weight pulls it down.

Bernedoodles with a curly coat are similar to the Poodle and will not shed. While there are no guarantees, even if you have serious allergies to dander, you should do well with a curly-coated Bernedoodle.

Breeders can often tell by the time a dog is a few weeks old what type of coat it will have, and can help match you to the best coat type for your situation.

If you are allergic to dog saliva, and your skin breaks out in hives when licked by a dog, you will most likely be allergic to all Bernedoodles regardless of coat type. If you still want a dog, a smaller dog produces less saliva than a larger one.

Since there are no absolute guarantees with coat type, responsible breeders will give you some time to see if you are allergic to your puppy and will allow you to return the pup if it is not working out.

As for grooming, the curlier the dog's coat, the harder it is to maintain. Since most Bernedoodles shed little, if at all, they need to be brushed regularly to prevent matting, and must be clipped every few months.

One Size Does Not Fit All

Bernedoodles come in different sizes, depending on the parents and the vagaries of genetics. Females are usually smaller than males.

A Standard Bernedoodle, which results from crossing a Standard Poodle with a Bernese Mountain Dog, will generally be 50 pounds and up, and around 23-29 inches at the shoulder. Most standards are in the 70-90 pound range.

A Mini Bernedoodle, which results from crossing a Miniature Poodle with a Bernese Mountain Dog, generally ranges from 25-49 pounds and is 18-22 inches at the shoulder.

A Tiny Bernedoodle, which results from crossing a Toy Poodle with a Mini Bernedoodle, ranges from 10-24 pounds and is about 12-17 inches at the shoulder.

These ranges capture the averages, but sometimes a pup will fall outside the expected height and weight. With hybrids, sometimes even a breeder is surprised!

In terms of temperament, Mini and Tiny Bernedoodles may have a slightly higher energy level than the standard, to reflect the same in the Miniature and Toy Poodle parent. However, a breeder who uses calm poodles, regardless of size, can produce docile Bernedoodles.

In my experience, smaller Bernedoodles tend to grow more quickly in the early months and then slow down. Standards continue to grow longer, and are slower to mature overall, as is typical of all larger dogs.

Different Generations

F1 – is a first generation cross, in which the pup is 50 per cent Bernese Mountain Dog and 50 per cent Poodle. The F1 cross is considered the healthiest, as the parents have the least likelihood of contributing genes for common inheritable diseases.

F1b – is a backcross in which a Bernedoodle is bred with a poodle. The puppy is 25 per cent Bernese, and 75 per cent Poodle. F1b puppies are the most likely to be non-shedding and allergy-friendly. Some breeders have backcrossed a Bernedoodle with a Bernese, which results in a dog with more of the Bernese traits. I prefer not to breed this backcross as there is a greater likelihood of shedding.

F2 – is a second-generation cross, in which an F1 Bernedoodle is crossed with another F1 Bernedoodle. This cross is again 50 per cent Bernese and 50 per cent Poodle. F2 crosses have more consistency in their lines.

F1 hybrids have the most variation in appearance, although most are a nice mix between the two parents. When you start breeding F2, F3 or F4 Bernedoodles, there will be more consistency in terms of the dogs' appearance. A breeder with "a look" in mind may start doing this.

If a breeder successively bred Bernedoodles 7 times (F7 Bernedoodle), and kept records of each breeding, he or she could apply to have it registered as a purebred dog with a registered kennel club.

The advantage of crossing Bernedoodles with other Bernedoodles is that it will give people a better sense of what they are likely to get, as with a purebred dog.

While first generation Bernedoodles have more variation in appearance, an experienced breeder will be able to give you an idea of what the pup will look like as an adult, based on what the parents have produced in the past and what traits they see in the pup.

The disadvantage of breeding generation after generation is that you are now doubling up on genetic traits and getting away from the hybrid vigor that makes a crossbreed special in the first place.

Here for a Good Time—*and* a Long Time

As a breed, the Bernedoodle is still young, so there is little to go on in terms of longevity and health concerns. What I do know is that of the approximately 400 Bernedoodles I have bred in the past decade, only one owner has reported a genetic health concern, and it was not life-threatening. I have not seen a case of cancer in my Bernedoodle lines since I started breeding them in 2003. It appears that hybrid vigor is indeed at play in creating a healthy dog that will be with you for a long time. At this point, I can only estimate an average lifespan. I predict that Standard Bernedoodles will live 12-15 years, Mini Bernedoodles up to 17 years and Tiny Bernedoodles up to 18 years. Usually, the smaller the dog the longer it lives.

While Bernedoodles tend to be healthier than their parent breeds, they can still be prone to conditions such as hip and elbow dysplasia and certain eye problems. Skin problems, such as hot spots and allergies, are also seen in this mix. Like any other breed of dog, they can get cancer.

Genetic testing can reduce the risk of many diseases. A reputable breeder will perform a number of tests and provide evidence of the successful results. You can read more about what to look for in a breeder in Chapter 5. It's important for prospective buyers to understand that breeders invest a great deal of money upfront in finding healthy breeding stock and doing the required testing. This investment is usually reflected in the higher cost of the puppy for the buyer. A higher upfront cost will most likely reduce vet bills down the road.

Is the Bernedoodle "Just Right" for Everyone?

I believe the Bernedoodle is a suitable dog for most people, but it's important to note that it is a very social dog that thrives on plenty of human interaction. While this hybrid is usually ideal for someone with allergies, its low- to non-shedding coat does mean more time, effort, and money spent on grooming. Lastly, if your Bernedoodle should happen to inherit the higher energy of the Poodle or the stubbornness of the Bernese—or both!—it will need more of your attention in the form of exercise and training, especially in the first couple of years.

> **An owner says…** *If you want a low-maintenance dog (both from a grooming and attention stand-point), a Bernedoodle may not be right you. They are extremely loving but also attention-seeking! Also, the fluffy and cuddly fur coat mats easily and is not for those that want a no-maintenance look. Because they are smart, they will challenge you, and a "lazy" owner may become frustrated by their antics.*

But if you have the time and enthusiasm, I predict your Bernedoodle will become the best friend you ever had—at least of the canine variety.

An owner says… *I wish I had known how much I was going to LOVE them. They are a wonderful combination of fun and smarts and they make fabulous family members… Bernedoodles are just like a snack mix that has all my favorite snacks mixed together… they are all awesome!*

Chapter 2

A Look Back at the Long and (Somewhat) Tortured Path

I was 15 years old, and living on a farm near Beaverton, Ontario, when I decided I wanted to breed dogs for a living. After a long campaign to get my mother on board, I bought a Golden Retriever named Lacey and put my plan into motion.

Although I loved Lacey and sold every pup she produced, I soon realized that Golden Retrievers were becoming a little too common. If I wanted to make a living doing what I loved, I would need to carve out a niche of my own.

That realization happened to coincide with my falling head over heels for a Bernese Mountain Dog, the first I'd ever seen. I was so besotted that I spent a long, hot summer mucking out horse stalls to earn the money for a Bernese of my own. My parents thought there were better things I could do with $1,500, namely save for college. But they were also well aware of my passion for dogs—and my "determination," to put it mildly. By fall, Mocca, a stunning Bernese, had joined my pack of two. She was everything I'd hoped for and more. I figured if people were willing to wait months for a Bernese from a reputable breeder, this might be the breed that would help me stand out.

Lacey and Mocca were both sweet and loving, but their temperaments differed in notable ways. Earnest, bright and eager to please, Lacey loved everyone indiscriminately. Mocca was more reserved and was somewhat shy with strangers. A gentle, sensitive soul, she sometimes needed to be persuaded to do what I asked. I considered her more self-possessed than stubborn, but there was no denying she was harder to train than Lacey. What Mocca lacked in tractability, however, she made up for in good looks and deep affection.

My goal was to breed both my girls to purebred partners, sell the puppies, and earn my way through college. Seeing my commitment and early success, my parents supported my goal.

It was all coming together except for one thing: my mom had terrible allergies, and she liked a clean house. While she allowed me to have the dogs, they had to live in an outdoor kennel. About this, she was adamant.

I started scheming. If I could breed low-shedding dogs that didn't trigger my mom's allergies, obviously she'd have to relent and welcome my pack inside. Further, I knew that she couldn't be the only allergy-prone, house-proud dog owner around. If I discovered a cute, good-natured, *hypoallergenic* dog, it might fill a marketable niche.

As I researched non-shedding breeds, I became intrigued by hybrids in general and poodle crosses in particular. It seemed that the poodle brought intelligence and playfulness to every mix, and also reduced or eliminated shedding. Better yet, crossing two purebreds tended to produce a healthier dog.

One fairly new hybrid that stood out was the Goldendoodle. There were several breeders in the United States and Australia, but as far as I could tell, only one in Canada at that time. I decided to give it a try.

Enter Dawson, the silver Standard Poodle. He was a prancing, energetic clown, and unquestionably the smartest of my little pack. I matched him with Lacey, and the resulting 12 Goldendoodles puppies were sweet bundles of gold or black fluff.

I had expected them to sell as quickly as my purebred Golden Retrievers, but people weren't used to paying much for crossbreeds. I had to convince them that these would be low-shedding, loving, highly trainable dogs that would probably be healthier than their parents. In short, I had to *sell* them. It worked, and before long, word spread about this great hybrid and they began to sell themselves.

In only one way was my experiment a failure: despite my success in producing a low-shedding dog for house-proud allergy sufferers, my mom still refused to allow dogs in the house!

Gaining Credentials

My breeding business picked up steam surprisingly quickly, and I wasn't thrilled about interrupting it for college. My parents kept up the pressure, and since I had enjoyed volunteering for my mentor, Dr. Rick Doner, at Beaverton Crossroads Veterinary Services, I decided to enroll in St. Lawrence College's Veterinary Technologist's program.

By that time, I had eight breeding dogs, and was focusing on producing both Goldendoodles and purebred Bernese Mountain Dogs. My dad looked after my pack during the week, when I was in Kingston. I'd leave on Monday morning at 5 a.m. and come home on Friday evening to be with my dogs over the weekend. The six-hour round trip never bothered me because I hated being away from my dogs. When a problem came up, however, I had to get creative. For example, when Mocca failed to produce enough milk to feed one of her litters, the pups commuted with me. I hid them in my dorm room for weeks and bottle-fed them between classes. It was a relief when they "graduated."

> **Did you know that…** Bernese Mountain Dogs are not the best moms in the canine universe? Their puppies often need special care and handling.

Trying a New Hybrid

I was still in college when my clients started suggesting I cross the Bernese Mountain Dog with the Standard Poodle. These people were mostly devoted Bernese fans who had become disheartened by the health problems of their favorite breed. They were looking for a way to keep the traits they loved about the Bernese while improving their odds of a longer life together.

Initially, I rejected the idea. An Internet search failed to turn up a single reference to this hybrid, so I assumed the market for them would be small. When I began breeding, I had made a commitment to myself that I would never breed a dog I wasn't sure I could sell to a good home. It would break my heart if any of my pups ended up in a shelter.

Eventually, however, so many people asked about Bernese crosses that I got curious myself. In 2003, I decided to try one litter of what I dubbed the "Bernedoodle." The litter consisted of two black puppies, each with a touch of white. Although I sold them without any trouble, I still wasn't convinced the demand was there and didn't try another litter for a couple of years.

Building a Better Goldendoodle

After graduating, I turned down a great job offer in favor of pursuing breeding full-time. I established SwissRidge Kennels in my home in Oakwood, Ontario. Finally, I could bring my dogs inside!

Since Goldendoodles had taken off, I focussed all my efforts on producing the best in this hybrid mix. I now had enough experience and education to realize I still had much to learn about breeding. That's when I got serious about research and development. I investigated lines many generations back, and began looking for breeding stock that would meet my rising standards.

It is a challenge for any breeder to find high quality breeding stock, but even more so for breeders of hybrid dogs. Many breeders of purebreds are so committed to protecting the integrity of their breed that they prefer not to sell dogs to those who intend to crossbreed them.

Over time, I have managed to build strong relationships with some of the best breeders of purebreds in the world. This is no small feat for a hybrid breeder. I made it a top priority to gain access to many unique lines of genetically sound, well-bred dogs—in short, to find dogs that are worthy of breeding. For me, that means great genes, a balanced temperament and good looks.

My belief is that there is a place for hybrid dogs, just as there is for purebreds. There will always be people who prefer to own a purebred dog, whether it's a Bernese or a Jack Russell Terrier. With a purebred, you know within certain parameters what you are going to get. You have a good idea of its size, its temperament, and its appearance. The best examples of a breed end up in the show ring, where they are judged on their look. A dog must have the right colors and conformation to compete.

I understand that approach. When it comes to Golden Retrievers, Standard Poodles, and Bernese Mountain Dogs, I probably have as critical an eye as many breeders of purebred dogs. I look for certain proportions, lines, and coloring. In fact, my breeding dogs might very well win in a show ring, if that were my objective.

At one time, they did. Until about 2006, I regularly showed my breeding dogs and had some Canadian Champions. I suppose I still felt I had something to prove to the purebred breeding establishment, which can sometimes be very critical of hybrid breeders. I don't feel that way anymore. My priorities shifted as my list of happy clients grew. I am completely satisfied with my decision to breed hybrids.

As noted earlier, my dogs are bred to be fun-loving companions. That is their only job. Many purebreds, on the other hand, were created to do very specific jobs. Terriers, for example, were bred to kill rodents. Sheepdogs were bred to herd. Retrievers, and many other dogs, were bred to hunt and retrieve. The very traits and drives that humans selected for in breeding over the generations have created an animal that may not be the ideal pet for the average family. Few of us have flocks we need to tend, prey we need to hunt, or vermin we need to rid from the family home. Sheepdogs, beagles and terriers have loads of character, but also a strong drive to work, and hunt. If that drive isn't given an outlet, it can lead to behavioural problems. In short, a purebred isn't always the best choice for someone who just wants to amble around the park for an hour before cuddling up with her dog to read a good book.

I let my clients guide my work, and they have been clear about their expectations. They want smart, active, goofy dogs that also know how to relax. They want healthy dogs that are going to be around a long time. And they want dogs that don't shed much, if at all.

Once I understood what my clients really wanted—the perfect companion dog—I could target my breeding efforts more precisely. Creating dogs to fill that niche has been my life's work to date, and I'm very pleased with how closely Goldendoodles and Bernedoodles hit the mark.

My goal is to breed dogs you can live with. While the people who come to me do care about their dog's appearance, they also prioritize health and personality. They want a character, a family member, a best friend. My approach must be working, because more and more people are coming back for a second dog, or even a third.

Breeders as Inventors

All professional breeders strive to improve their lines, but those who breed hybrids have more room to experiment. My dogs need only conform to my expectations—not those of breed organizations. They don't need to be a certain size, shape, or color to make it into a show ring, and I am free to focus on the traits that matter to me in creating a perfect companion dog.

To that end, I deliberately select parent dogs that have desirable traits consistent with my goal of creating happy, affectionate, low-shedding family pets. I avoid breeding dogs with traits that are *not* consistent with that goal. For example, I choose Golden Retrievers and Poodles with a low prey drive because they aren't likely to be working in the field. Further, I choose Poodles that are playful, but not hyper. And I work very hard to find Bernese Mountain Dogs that are calm and affectionate, not skittish.

> **Did you know that…** A dog's temperament is just as much a result of genetics as its coloring? That's why it's essential to have the perfect match of calm, stable parents.

It's not often possible to assess temperament many generations back, so when purchasing breeding stock, I have to rely on the word of reputable breeders. Once I confirm that we share the same high standards, I can be confident that my chances of getting a stable dog are high. Of course, the dogs also need to be healthy and pass all the key tests that indicate they're unlikely to have the genes for common problems in their breed.

And beyond all that, they still have to be gorgeous. By gorgeous, I don't mean show-ring perfect. I simply mean that they have to be pleasing to the eye. Frankly, I want my dogs to be so attractive that people stop their owners to admire them. And it happens all the time.

> **An owner says…** *Everyone asks about her in the street, and people ask if they can buy her from us.*

Tough Choices

Even when prospective breeding dogs meet all my criteria, I still have to make careful decisions about the best pairings. I may match a great Poodle with a great Golden Retriever and, for whatever reason, the resulting puppies may be merely… average. Average is not good enough. I want my dogs to have it all. And if they don't, I move on to new parents.

I believe breeders should be just as diligent about producing a quality hybrid as a purebred. That means research and significant up front investment. Because many good breeders will not sell their dogs to someone with a hybrid breeding program, I have had to be resourceful in locating quality breeding stock. This requires travelling to many different countries and visiting hundreds of kennels to find Golden Retrievers, Poodles, and Bernese Mountain Dogs that not only have a great pedigree, but also the look and the temperament I demand. I've been fortunate to cultivate relationships with excellent breeders who see the value in hybrids.

Despite my research and investment, some of the dogs I buy as puppies with the intention of breeding do not mature as I would hope. They may not pass their health clearances, despite excellent pedigrees. Their temperament may not be quite right. Or their conformation may not meet my specifications. If for any reason, I have doubts about a dog's capacity to produce pups to my standards, they don't make it into my breeding program. Instead, they are altered and go to good homes.

Even when a dog seems ideal, and makes the cut for my breeding program, I scrutinize the resulting pups carefully. If a dog produces a pup with a genetic disease twice, the parent is retired. That choice is straightforward, but often I am concerned with nuances. If, for example, several owners from the same litter contact me to say that their dogs are "extremely active," I am unlikely to breed the parent dogs again. Instead, I will try them with other mates. If I'm dissatisfied with the next litter, the dog is retired.

These are not easy decisions. I love all my dogs, and more importantly, the pups I produce are beloved by their owners even if they are not flawless to my critical eye. But I believe that all breeders need to look at their dogs and acknowledge faults. It takes a certain type of person to be able to do that. I've had to remove many wonderful dogs from my breeding program because something wasn't quite right. Some breeders may be able to ignore that one small thing, but I have set my standards for my program high. As a breeder, I'm an unapologetic perfectionist. Indeed, my standards seem to increase every year as I take what I learn and apply it to the next litter.

Luckily, there are some truly perfect matches that consistently produce very special puppies. When that magic happens, I repeat the breeding several times. The proof is in the fact that many owners will wait until I breed that pair again to buy their second dog, because they are so delighted with their first.

Gold Standard for Goldendoodles

It took many years to nail my strategy for breeding hybrids via the Goldendoodles, and become confident in the full range I produce— including Goldendoodles, English Goldendoodles, standards, mediums/miniatures, and tiny versions in a nice array of colors.

That commitment gained the attention of Animal Planet's TV show, *Breeder of the Pack*. The producer who contacted me said they wanted to profile breeders "at the top of their game." I was flattered, but initially reluctant to invest the amount of time required to shoot a half-hour episode. Even then, time was in very short supply. However, I decided it was a good opportunity to give my clients some insight into life at SwissRidge Kennels, including my charitable work. Equally important, it was a chance to showcase the advantages of the hybrid, something *Breeder of the Pack* had not done before.

The six long days of shooting turned out to be a great experience. I was so pleased with the result that I agreed to promote the show on several TV and radio shows, in the company of several unruly puppies. (Links ˌ episode are posted on my website.)

At the time of shooting, in 2011, I was ramping up my breeding of Bernedoodles and had a cute litter available to take a starring turn. This drew attention to my new hybrid, which was both welcome and daunting. I already knew that breeding Bernedoodles was an entirely different ballgame from Goldendoodles, with new rules and more complicated players.

Fortunately, I like a challenge.

Chapter 3

In retrospect, it's lucky that my work as a breeder progressed as it did. Had I started my career by trying to breed the perfect Bernedoodle, well… I might be working as a veterinary technician in a lab right now. In fact, breeding Bernedoodles has made me very grateful for my education, and confirms my commitment to keeping my certification in good standing.

Goldendoodles are relatively easy to breed. Both Golden Retrievers and Poodles tend to get pregnant easily, and are good moms. As long as a breeder does her homework, the results are reasonably predictable. Most Goldendoodle buyers want a dog that resembles a Golden Retriever, with a teddy bear look, a stocky build, and a low- to non-shedding coat. This is straightforward to produce. If you breed a Golden Retriever to a blonde, apricot, or red Poodle, the puppies will almost always be blonde, apricot, or red, because the dogs have the same genetic color makeup.

Similarly, Bernedoodle buyers want their dogs to resemble a Bernese, with a tri-color coat that is low- to non-shedding. There is no question that the tri-color of the Berner is a huge part of the Bernedoodle's appeal. Unfortunately, it is extremely difficult to achieve, as the Bernese and the Poodle have totally different color genotypes. The results are far from predictable, and as a result, those who are dead set on getting a Bernedoodle that looks just like the Bernese Mountain Dog usually face a long wait.

Bernedoodles are not easy to breed, and while I'm producing more and more tri-colored puppies, they don't come easily or consistently.

With each litter, my hope is the same: to see a series of healthy little creatures that replicate the exact coloring of the Bernese Mountain Dog. I like to see a jet black base color, a deep rich brown above the eyes, on the cheeks and chest, under the tail and on the legs. All the better if there is white in exactly the right places: a blaze on the forehead, a white muzzle and chest, tip of the tail and all four paws.

Don't get me wrong, though. If I'm anxious to produce tri-color Bernedoodles, it's because that's what the majority of my clients want. Personally, I don't discriminate. A Bernedoodle of any color is still as sweet. If I got too hung up on standards, it would diminish the fun of breeding hybrids. Indeed, it would be too much like the more rigid world of purebred breeding that I chose to leave behind.

I try to approach breeding from the viewpoint of an inventor. Every litter is a new opportunity and I learn from each one. Producing exactly what my clients want in a Bernedoodle is not a simple math equation I can solve. Genes are tricky even with purebreds; with hybrids they become a worthy opponent that keeps me constantly on my toes.

I always keep my priorities firmly in order. My first responsibility is to produce healthy, stable pups that bring joy to their families. If my pups don't have four white feet, it is hardly the end of the world. A big part of the hybrid's charm is that each dog is unique.

Built for All Seasons

There is more to a Bernedoodle than color, of course, and I aspire to a certain ideal in physique as well.

Obviously, some pups will take after the Poodle, and others the Bernese, but I prefer dogs that are a nice mix of the two. I particularly like to see the more agile body type of the Poodle in my Bernedoodles. Bernese Mountain Dogs are built solidly to withstand extreme winter conditions in the Swiss Alps. They were not bred to enjoy the summer activities most of my clients want to share with their canine companions. Bringing Poodle genes into the game improves the likelihood of the Bernedoodle being able to enjoy outdoor activities year-round.

It seems that nearly all Bernedoodles inherit the Berner's love of cold weather and snow. My own will play outside for hours and resist coming inside, even when covered with snow.

I've been happy to find that Bernedoodles tolerate hot weather much better than their Bernese ancestors. That said, they will be much happier on summer days if clipped down (See Chapter 13 for an example of an appropriate summer cut).

Many Bernedoodle owners claim to have the best of both worlds:

> *Marley and Gizmo both love the water. In fact, they are out-of-their-heads crazy about it. They are the same way about snow. They have the large Bernese Mountain Dog paws, which are webbed like a poodle's. So, they have built-in snowshoes and swim fins.*

While the majority of Bernedoodles seem to inherit a love of water from their Poodle parents, some do not.

> *Mojo doesn't like the water. She can swim, and will follow me in if I go, but will otherwise avoid it. She even walks WAY around puddles so that she doesn't get her paws wet!*

Overall, I aspire to a well-proportioned, intelligent, agile dog with the following characteristics:

- a soft gentle expression in dark brown, slightly oval-shaped eyes, with eyelids close fitting to the eye.
- ears set slightly above the eye that are triangular and of medium-length, in proportion to the head.
- a skull that is mainly flat and broad.
- a muzzle that is short and wide, and slightly longer than it is wide.
- black lips, nose, and eyelids, and tight-fitting lips.
- a complete set of 42 teeth, as adults, and a nice scissor bite.
- neck of medium length and flow at a slight angle into the back
- broad and stocky body, but less so than the Bernese.

- a body that is slightly longer than it is tall, with a straight top line and good depth in the chest.
- hindquarters that are muscular and strong, and neither too wide nor too narrow.
- forelegs that are straight with good substance.
- large and compact feet, without toes turning in or out.
- tail should be bushy and carried at mid-level in everyday activity (but I don't mind a curled tail—it shows character).
- an upward, forward carriage and prancing gait.
- a soft, wavy coat that is low- to non-shedding (curly coats mat more easily; straight coats are more likely to shed).

I do not like to see blue eyes, loose jowls, a sloping back, an improper bite, a long muzzle, or a wiry coat.

Did you know… that Bernedoodles are born with pink noses that gradually turn black by the time they are a few months old?

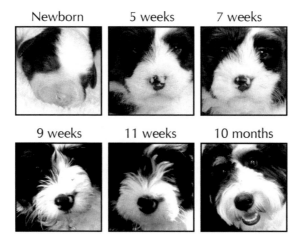

Newborn 5 weeks 7 weeks

9 weeks 11 weeks 10 months

The Problem with Bernese Mountain Dogs

There are plenty of fundamental challenges in producing Bernedoodles that make worrying about color something of a luxury.

Let's start with the basic fact that healthy Bernese Mountain Dogs with a sound temperament are extremely difficult to find. As I've noted, significant inbreeding resulted from bringing these dogs back from the brink of extinction. Adding to that challenge, I want a certain look in my breeding dogs. In particular, I like big, robust Berners with large, blocky heads.

I have forged relationships with a number of excellent breeders who are willing to sell their dogs into a hybrid breeding program. Also, in a great stroke of luck for me, my mother fell in love with the breed and has developed a very strong line of Berners that have what I consider to be the perfect look and temperament. Further, none of the dogs that I've purchased from my mom has ever failed its health clearances.

Finding great Berners is just the beginning of the challenge. It's been my experience that Bernese Mountain Dogs are difficult to breed, period. They have such erratic cycles that even with vigilant monitoring and impeccable timing, they may not get pregnant when expected. When they do, they may have small litters, and some have more trouble delivering pups than other breeds.

Then—and it pains me to say this—Bernese Mountain Dogs really are not the best moms. Some produce too little milk to raise a litter without intervention. Worse, they are not particularly delicate with their pups, and have been known to lie on them, with predictably heart-rending results.

In short, a breeder needs to keep a very close eye on her Bernese moms and be ready to jump in to look after the pups. Bottle feeding is more the norm than the exception.

The Problem with Poodles

Poodles bring their own challenges to the breeder-inventor in the form of complex and unreliable color genetics. What you see with a parent poodle (or its parents and grandparents) may not be what you will get in its offspring.

It would be reasonable to expect two white poodles, with white poodle ancestors, to produce similar pups when paired with a Bernese Mountain Dog. Regrettably, there is nothing reasonable about poodle color genetics. One of those white poodles might be harbouring a hidden surprise for its breeder. A gene, for example, that causes the colors of its Bernedoodle offspring to fade, or even disappear. Some of my Bernedoodle puppies have changed from black to silver, or lost the brown they had when they were born. It's difficult to predict how often these gremlin genes may surface in each litter. The potential for color change is often evident as early as eight weeks, but when the fading gene is involved, it may happen later, generally within the first year.

Color genetics both intrigue breeders and make them want to tear out their hair. DNA testing is becoming more common, but it is not yet 100% trustworthy for indicating exactly what coloring the dog will produce in pups.

That's challenging enough for breeders dedicated to producing Poodles. But when you are a breeder using a Poodle to produce a specific hybrid, it can be a frustrating puzzle, indeed.

It's probably safe to say that no breeder has Poodle color genetics completely mastered. As a result, the Bernedoodle with the perfect Bernese coloration and pattern will continue to be somewhat elusive despite a great deal of effort with design.

Try and Try Again

It is nearly impossible to find adult dogs for my breeding program that have the right lineage, genetics, and health clearances. That is why I need to start with puppies. I research all my lines back five generations, decide which breeder I want to purchase a puppy from, and specify the parents. Then, like anyone else, I have to wait for the litter to be born.

I raise the puppy until it is of breeding age, studying it the whole time to see how it is developing, and how it interacts with other dogs and people. By the time it's a year old, I know whether or not I like the puppy's temperament, and can proceed with the required health testing. Only at this point, perhaps two years or more from the time I first decide to buy a new breeding dog, am I ready to actually breed it.

Imagine how disappointing it is after all this time and investment, to find that the beautiful Poodle you've pinned such high hopes on has a sneaky little gene that throws off the coloring in a few of your carefully bred puppies. It happens all the time and is one of the biggest frustrations for a Bernedoodle breeder hoping to produce tri-colour dogs *that stay that way.*

It is truly a case of trial and error where color is concerned. Bernedoodle breeders just have to be honest with buyers when they know that there is a chance a pup's colours may fade or change. And the only way of knowing whether or not that is likely to happen is repeated breeding with a particular Poodle.

Bernedoodle buyers need to be aware that, because of unreliable poodle color genetics, breeders may not be able to give them an ironclad guarantee that their puppy's coloring will remain exactly as it appears at the age of eight weeks. But a breeder with experience and integrity will be upfront with clients about the chances of a pup's colors remaining fixed.

> **An owner says…** *Our pup's original color markings have faded as she has matured, leaving her more bi-colored than tri-colored, but she is still a beautiful, lovable addition to our family.*

I am working very hard to find the right combination, and an increasing number of my pups have the right colors and keep them. But as I learn, I remind myself that while a few owners have been disappointed when a pup's color changes, no one has been disappointed in its temperament.

Getting with the Program

To summarize, the biggest challenge I face in producing Bernedoodles is finding the right breeding stock. This is also difficult with Goldendoodles, but the stakes are higher with Bernedoodles. Because Bernese Mountain dogs can be stubborn and skittish, it's absolutely essential to find the most balanced dogs and pair them with a Poodle that is playful, but not hyper.

Finding the right dogs to breed is like a treasure hunt, and I study them carefully, hoping to discover in time that they are true jewels. Luckily, many people are willing to adopt my potential breeding dogs so that they have loving homes while they grow up. If they fit with my program, the dog visits my kennel to breed, and stays with its family the rest of the year. If it doesn't suit my breeding needs, it makes its home permanently with its adoptive family.

I am building my breeding line slowly and deliberately, and as it grows, I've been able to expand to mini-Bernedoodles and finally Tiny Bernedoodles.

WORLD'S FIRST TINY BERNEDOODLE LITTER!

An owner says… *I love the size of my tiny Bernedoodle… She is tri-coloured and has the greatest markings that just give her the most adorable look and facial expressions. Everywhere I take her I get compliments on her appearance and everyone asks what breed she is. She is just plain happy all the time… She seems to like playing with larger breed dogs… I think she believes she is a big dog trapped in a small dog's body.*

For my Bernedoodle backcrosses and Tiny Bernedoodles, I keep pups from my own litters, applying the same rigorous standards to them. I look at body type, colour, personality, how they interact with me and where they rank in their litter. They must have a proper bite, no hernia, and no heart murmur. I also like to see a wavy coat, because a curly coat is more inclined to mat.

Breeding Bernedoodles requires constant research and decisions based largely on experience, but also a bit of intuition. It all takes time, and I'll admit that it can be frustrating, as it means I need to keep people waiting for puppies longer than I might like. On the bright side, it's forcing me to develop patience—something that is not part of *my* genetic make-up.

Chapter 4

An Exceptional Litter

A breeder can learn something from every litter, but every so often, one comes along that takes you a dramatic step forward in your understanding. For me, that litter was born in November 2011 to Gemini, a Bernese Mountain Dog, by Dolce, a chocolate Standard Poodle.

I had high hopes for this pairing, both in terms of coloring and temperament. Gemini, 85 pounds at age three, was bred at SwissRidge, and had already produced Bernedoodle pups for me. A typical Berner, Gemini is very loving, but has a hint of stubbornness, too. She has an energy level that is slightly higher than the average Berner's, but is always happy just to hang out with me.

Dolce was fresh out of the gate—just a year old, and recently cleared for breeding. A social butterfly, he's playful, goofy, fun, and active, and I was very much looking forward to seeing the pups he'd produce.

Call it breeder's intuition, but something told me to check on Gemini late one night, and sure enough she had already produced one puppy. It was still in its sac, and nearly died. I revived the little female, and in my cupped hands was a beautiful tri-colored Bernedoodle. While I had produced other tri-colored pups, this was the first one with white on its face. I remember looking down at this tiny girl and thinking, "She's perfect, and she's mine."

That was Gucci, and she's still mine, as I may use her for breeding one day.

For the rest of the night, I sat at Gemini's side, helping to deliver nine more pups. I was excited to see that all had beautiful markings, though none came as close to the Bernese as Gucci. I was thrilled with this litter, knowing I had come so much closer to the look I wanted in a Bernedoodle. Dolce had done very well.

It took work to keep this litter alive. Gemini, like most Berners, did not have enough milk to feed all her pups, so I bottle fed them every few hours. I also had to give them fluids under the skin for the first week to keep them hydrated. The work paid off, as all of them thrived, including the runt, Gizmo, who had to be hand-raised because his littermates picked on him. As an adult, Gizmo surpassed his father in size and rivals his mother.

> **Did you know...** that a hybrid dog may mature to be larger than either parent?

A Study in Hybrid Diversity

Describing this litter from Gemini and Dolce will showcase just how different hybrid siblings may be. In fact, you may find it hard to believe they all have the same parents. Check my website for more photos of this litter.

Let's take a look.

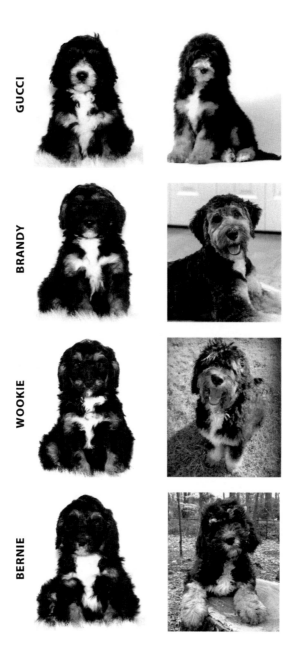

Male #1—Bernie

My observations: I judged this male to be an average, middle-of-the road puppy, who was fun, happy, and affectionate. He was good in new situations. On the temperament test, he scored 3.4. (Note: I'll discuss temperament testing further in Chapter 6, but will say here that pups are scored out of 6, with 1 being the boldest and 6 being the most timid. My pups generally fall in the 3-4 range).

His owner says… Bernie is 120 pounds, with a thick, wavy coat that does not mat easily.

> *He's quite a character. He's just one big, happy muppet. If he were a human, he'd be walking around with a big smile on his face all the time. He is smart as a whip, but pretty stubborn… He's a very spunky young man…Maybe he's slowed down a tad, but not a whole bunch.*

> *He's the best dog I've ever had and there have been seven, of various breeds. Still a head-turner. People call him the gentle giant because he's so massive yet so sweet.*

> *He brings all his toys and bones under his favorite tree. Whenever something is missing from the house, we look under Bernie's tree and voila.*

Male #2—Dexter

My observations: This pup was more laid back than his siblings—even a little lazy. He would sit and watch the others instead of engaging all the time. He didn't pick fights, and was the first to leave them. I scored him at 3.6.

His owner says… Dexter is 83 pounds and has a wavy coat that doesn't shed, but requires a fair bit of work to maintain.

> *I love Dexter's personality! He is the biggest goof and so cuddly—always wanting to be by my side… Dexter is so loving. He loves to jump up on*

to the couch and try to squish between my husband and me... He brings us presents all the time, shoes, toys etc., but has never been a chewer—just likes to bring them to us, drop them on the floor then jump up on the couch! He is great with other dogs and other people and not scared or timid.

He is definitely settling down. It's amazing how fast it happened! He is so relaxed about everything in life that it's a good reminder to me to do the same. I have never heard him growl at anything—human, dog or otherwise. There isn't a possessive bone in his body, but he sure loves to be near you. I don't have to worry about him running away because he's always within eye contact distance. He's happy as long as he knows we're around. He is also a huge cuddler! I tried to train him to cuddle because that is what I wanted — a furry friend to keep me company. He is my best friend and I couldn't ask for a better one!

Male #3—Wookie

My observations: Typical, middle-of-the-road pup, who loves people and other dogs. I scored him at 3.4.

His owner says... Wookie is 90 pounds, and has a wavy coat that mats easily if it gets too long.

Wookie is a delightful dog that makes us laugh and smile every day... He loves everyone and everything he meets. Essentially he is a big, goofy ball of love. He has such a great personality and is quite clever. He is also a great communicator. If he is hungry he will bring us his bowl, or flip it on the ground so we can hear that he is hungry. He is great with both of our kids.

Wookie has a solid temperament. He is not aggressive in any way. He can be stubborn and have his own ideas of what he wants to do. He does what we call 'the protest' when he doesn't like something and rolls on his back in defiance.

It must be the poodle in him, but he likes to climb. He goes on the kids' play-set—up the ladder and down the slide. He perches on stools and in chairs like a circus dog.

Male #4—Chester

My observations: This was one of the more active pups—fun, playful, and always the first to try things. Curious and adventurous, he was the first to come up to me in the mornings—a clear leader. He scored 3 on the temperament test.

His owner says: Chester is 105 pounds. He has a wavy coat with some curl, and minimal shedding.

Chester is healthy and loved by all both in and out of our house. He's lovable, kind, sweet, attention-seeking, goofy and HAPPY! … He's very rambunctious. Also he will eat anything, so his goat-like appetite has cost us some money in vet bills.

Every day is a story with Chester! … When he's in the car with me he has to be "shotgun" and he literally sits on his haunches and reclines with his one arm out the window! It's hilarious! I've been stopped by other drivers to ask about him. I have a great dog in Chester. I hope and pray he's with me for a long time. He's brought nothing but happiness (well, sometimes frustration!)… You couldn't have picked a better dog for our family.

Male #5—Gizmo

My observations: Gizmo was the smallest male and I had to take him away and raise him myself. I don't really know how he interacted with the litter as he was with me all the time. But he was a very affectionate, calm, and content puppy. He scored 3.4 on the temperament test. (Note: his owner also owns Marley, female #2 of the same litter)

His owner says… Gizmo weighs 80 pounds. He has a large, wide head, a deep chest, and long, elegant legs. He prances like a Poodle when he's happy. He can leap quite high over obstacles from a standing position. His coat is wavy and soft; it is easy to brush and does not mat easily.

My two sibling Bernedoodles have similarities and differences. They are both intelligent, fun-loving, affectionate, extremely loyal, adventurous, trusting, and always ready to try something new.

Where they differ is in their energy level: the male is moderate energy, while the female is high energy. Also, the male has more of the steady nature of the Bernese Mountain Dog; when we hike, he prefers to stay with the group at a moderate pace, while his sister would rather chase every squirrel and follow every scent, dashing ahead and around us at a headlong run, then 'checking in' before dashing off again.

I am more deeply bonded with Gizmo than I have ever been with a dog. He is very sweet and gentle with me and loves to sit by my side.

He is mellow, but not low-energy, and now quite settled down. He can also be very playful and goofy, and loves to roughhouse with my husband.

My dogs' temperament is comparable in many ways to the Bernese Mountain Dog: steady, intelligent, and snow-loving... Their activity level is higher than the average Bernese, especially during the warmer months because they don't seem so bothered by the heat. They are very intelligent, but their intelligence must be channelled through (moderate) training, or they may find outlets for their intelligence that are not appreciated by their owners. They learn commands more quickly than any other dog I've had. In fact, Marley and Gizmo are halfway to earning their American Kennel Club Canine Good Citizen titles.

Female #1—Brandy

My observations: Middle-of-the-road, typical puppy. Fun, happy, playful, loves people, and good in new situations. She rated 3.4 on the temperament test.

Her owner says… Brandy is 51 pounds, has a beautiful soft coat with loose curls that mat easily.

She is extremely smart, probably the smartest dog I have ever had. She adores people and is very social. She is very affectionate and loves people. She has a high energy level, but settles down when in the house. She needs a calm, firm demeanor when you are training her because she gets very excited.

Female #2—Marley

My observations: This was another active pup—fun, playful, loving, and quick to try new things. Curious and daring, she was always one of the first to come and see me. She scored 3 on the temperament test. (Note: Marley was returned to me by her first owner at eight months, and had received very little training. Gizmo's owner adopted her soon afterwards.)

Her owner says… Marley weighs 72 pounds and is lean and built more like a poodle. She has shorter legs, longer body, and is very, very athletic. Her coat is thicker and curlier than her brother's and tends to form mats quickly.

Marley has the most amazingly exuberant personality I've ever seen in a dog, and it was important that we didn't break that while breaking her bad habits. She does everything with such joyful exuberance: cuddling, running, eating, etc., which makes up for the extra work. She will be an amazing dog when she grows up!

We adopted Marley at eight months… I assume Marley didn't have much structure or many rules. That, plus high energy, plus a highly dominant personality equals a pup that is a handful. On the other hand, she really wants to please, so that works to my advantage. She's not the easiest dog, but I LOVE her. She is the most loving, playful, and affectionate dog I've ever had. We just have to channel her energy in the right direction.

Marley recently won First Place during graduation from her Obedience class. She also won "Longest Sit-Stay" a couple of weeks ago. She loved the classes and was always on her best behavior. (Now, if we could duplicate the results at home, I'd be thrilled.)

Marley loves to retrieve. Ball, Frisbee, stick, whatever. On land or in water. She is also great at catching the ball or Frisbee in the air.

Both Marley and Gizmo LOVE the water. Marley usually wants to retrieve, and she swims fast and with purpose. She swims very low in the water, with just her forehead and the top of her muzzle and nose above the water. Gizmo, on the other hand, just loves to be in the water… he slips into the water, and hangs there totally relaxed… kind of like a jellyfish, I suppose.

Female #3—Sophie

My observations: middle-of-the-road, your typical puppy. Fun, happy, playful, loves people and other dogs. She was a social puppy and good in new situations. I ranked her 3.4 on the temperament scale.

Her Owner says… Sophie weighs 65 pounds, and has a wavy overcoat with a dense undercoat that needs a lot of work to maintain.

She is soft, tractable, goofy, people-centric, and responsive to training. She is also dog-shy and wolfs down her food… We were looking for a soft companion dog with some good size and smarts, and in that light we got everything we were looking for. Well, maybe not brain-surgeon smart, but average to above in the dog world.

She has settled down a lot now… Most common description is 'sweet and silly.' She loves to flop down in puddles, but hasn't got her feet off the bottom in deep water.

Female #4—Lacey

My observations: This one was the smallest female of the litter. Although she scored a 3.4 on the temperament test, I noticed she was squirmy most of the time. She seemed very active, playful, tail always wagging and could not sit still. I think she wore the other pups out with her play. She was small but feisty and could hold her own. She would play with her littermates like she was bigger than them. The difference between Lacey and Gizmo, who were the same size, is that Lacey stood up to her littermates, whereas Gizmo would have died if I hadn't removed him. Although Lacey scored average on the temperament test, I could see she was very spunky. I took all factors into account and made sure she had an owner who could handle a little firecracker.

Her owner says… Lacey is 62 lbs, with a curly coat—no shedding, but a lot of work to maintain if left long. If short then there is no real maintenance for the coat.

Lacey is very very active. We have had her in obedience class or some other form of classes since we got her. Lacey can be timid or unsure of new things until she does them… She loves all people and dogs and very much wants to play.

As for personality, Lacey is the sweetest dog you could ever meet. She is happy, loving and just wonderful. She loves being around people and will push right into you to get some attention. She often will sit on your feet or lean up against the back of your legs just so that she can be touching you. She is also very soft. She doesn't like to have someone raise their voice at her and really needs to be treated kindly… Honestly, I wouldn't want her to be any other way and feel that her sweet kind nature is a very good thing.

Lacey is incredibly smart and picks things up very quickly. I have never had an issue with teaching her a new thing… Due to her high energy she isn't interested in doing things she does not deem fun to do. This requires that people are patient with her and that most activities be rewarded if you want her to perform them… She'll ignore you if she doesn't want to do what you are asking and thinks she can get away with it.

Female #5—Gucci

My observations: Fun, active, playful, puppy that loves people and other dogs. Affectionate but still curious and independent. Social, and good in new situations. I ranked her as 3.4, and decided she was a perfect match… for me!

Her owner says… Gucci is about 70 pounds. She had a wavy coat as a pup, but now it is curly, and it does mat if not brushed regularly.

Gucci is fun, goofy, and playful. She loves people and other dogs. She has lots of spunk and energy to burn. Despite being an intact female, Gucci is not dominant toward other females. She is very smart and well-behaved. She loves to run and play, but she also respects other dogs and us, and is very obedient. She is calm in the house and loves to chill out.

Gucci is a perfect example of what I like about the Bernedoodle. She's goofy and playful, and very affectionate and loyal. When I look at her, I want to squeeze her cute little face. Not only does she have a great personality, she's stunning too, with a great color, build and coat.

Almost everything about Bernedoodles makes them perfect family dogs. However, they do mature slower than Goldendoodles and they can be stubborn. That said, there are many breeds far more stubborn than the Bernedoodle.

A Turning Point

I was—and still am—very happy with this litter. I'm thrilled they've fit so well into their permanent homes. As large dogs, they have a ways to go before they are fully mature. When they settle down after the age of two, their owners will be even happier.

As a breeder, I can't ask for more.

Except I still do. It's probably not in my nature to be fully satisfied, as far as my work is concerned. Like any inventor, it's the journey I enjoy. I take a moment to savor successes, and then move ahead.

So while I bred Gemini to Dolce once more, and produced a second fine litter of pups that are well-loved by their owners, I have since retired Dolce to a wonderful home where he's living the good life.

Dolce took me much closer to the look I wanted in a Bernedoodle, but that's only one part of the equation. I also aim to produce dogs with moderate energy levels. When matched with a placid Golden Retriever, Dolce produced calm pups. When matched with Gemini—a higher energy dog than the average Berner—Dolce produced more active pups. Things may have been different if Dolce were matched with a different Berner, but I decided to forge on. It was one of the tougher decisions I've had to make in developing my line.

But Dolce certainly isn't complaining.

Chapter 5

So, you still want a Bernedoodle?

Now we have seen the extreme variation that can occur within a first generation (F1) Bernese Mountain Dog-Standard Poodle cross. The differences among pups will, as a rule, be greatest in an F1 cross, either standard or mini. In fact, the size variation can also be quite significant in the F1 Mini-Bernedoodle, with pups ranging from 25-49 pounds—and a few I've seen get bigger.

An F2 breeding—a Bernedoodle crossed with another Bernedoodle of the same size and color—will generally produce more consistency in size, physique, coat type and coloring. I suspect it may be possible to come closest to matching the perfect Bernese Mountain Dog coloring by crossing two beautifully marked Bernedoodles. However, successive generations tend to lose a little of that desirable hybrid vigour.

There will always be variation in hybrids—that's the nature of crossbreeding. But the variation will be more noticeable with a dog in the mix that is as striking in color as the Bernese. There are many possible combinations of colors and patterns.

Further, with Bernedoodles, it's entirely possible for one pup to mature to be more than double the size of its sibling. In the Gemini-Dolce litter profiled earlier, one dog weighs around 50 pounds, another is 120 pounds, and the others are spaced fairly evenly along the continuum between. Some have a moderate energy level, some high energy level, and their coats vary from non-shedding to moderate shedding. But all of them, according to their owners, are affectionate and bright.

Perhaps the major constants I've seen across all Bernedoodles are that they are loving, happy-go-lucky and clever. I don't think I've met a Bernedoodle that isn't above average in the canine brains department. It can be challenging to stay ahead of them, especially if they get a strong hit of the

Bernese stubbornness. They all have what it takes to be well-behaved canine companions, but you will need to put in the work to get them there.

An owner says: *[They] can be quite strong-willed. When you combine that with intelligence, you cannot pull too many tricks on these dogs. They, however, will outsmart you. Every. Single. Day.*

Breeders – the Good, the Bad and the Ugly

What is the aspiring Bernedoodle owner to do in the face of such diversity? The answer is simple: find an experienced, trustworthy breeder. It is always—*always*—important to have a responsible breeder who does all the appropriate health clearances and has an established record of producing dogs with a sound temperament. But if you are buying a hybrid, it is even more important to have a breeder with extensive knowledge and experience.

I've heard from many distressed dog owners who bought a dog from a "backyard" breeder, a pet store, or a puppy mill, and ended up with a pet that, however loveable, has serious health problems that rack up equally serious vet bills. This is particularly risky with a Bernese Mountain Dog in the mix, as quality breeding dogs are so hard to come by. Given the difficulty I have had in finding great Berners, the chances of a less conscientious breeder doing so are negligible.

Still, some people take shortcuts and learn some hard lessons at the hands of irresponsible breeders. I've known people to ask for a small hybrid and end up with a 'doodle the size of a horse, for example. Others were "guaranteed" a hypoallergenic dog, but ended up with a major shedder. The second situation may cause people to give up their dog, and since puppy mills aren't known for their return policies, this dog may not have a happily-ever-after.

Temperament is another huge issue in dubious breeding operations. Bernese that are not carefully bred can be skittish, obstinate, and even aggressive. Purebred Poodles can be frantically energetic and high strung. Many casual breeders are unaware, or unconcerned, that temperament is heavily controlled by genes, even in crossbreeds. They don't worry about the long-term. Unlike professional breeders, whose reputations hang in the balance if their dogs don't do well over the long haul, casual or disreputable breeders only need to care whether a puppy is cute enough to make a quick sale.

And finally, socialization. Your neighbour, who, on a whim, mates her Bernese with the Poodle down the block, may do a fine job of socializing the pups, but it won't be enough to compensate for unwanted traits a parent dog contributes to the mix. As for puppy mills, the parents and the pups receive no socialization at all. The breeding dogs live in inhumane conditions that keep them under constant stress, and stress affects puppies even before they are born. Such pups don't stand a fighting chance of becoming well-balanced, happy dogs.

Suffice it to say that the puppy you buy from a puppy mill—often via a pet store—is unlikely to fulfill your hopes for a stable, healthy family member. Many will end up being re-homed because things didn't work out, for any number of reasons.

Many people simply do not realize the risk they are taking in buying a puppy from a backyard breeder, a pet store, or a puppy mill. They may overestimate the power of socialization and training to counteract careless breeding. They may underestimate the power of a strong genetic foundation to produce the results they want.

Assuming the result you want is a healthy, happy dog that will be with you for more than a decade, it's important to do your research and invest appropriately.

Puppies from a reputable breeder tend to cost more because of the breeder's investment in research and development, running necessary tests that produce solid lines, and operating a quality kennel.

> **An owner says...** *We chose a Bernedoodle as we were looking for a dog with the temperament of a Bernese, the smarts of a Poodle, and of course minimal to no shedding. Temperament was the priority as we wanted a dog that was friendly and full of love, not just to our family, but to friends, strangers and other animals. Our expectations were very high and we knew we would not get all we wanted, however to our delight our expectations were not just met, they were surpassed. Our Bernedoodle is simply perfect.*

I would go so far as to say that breeders who sell a dog to a pet store simply don't care about the welfare of their pups. And that is a very bad sign indeed.

Profile of a Responsible Breeder

It bears repeating: responsible breeders care about their pups and where they are going.

A good breeder will perform all health clearances listed below and will share health certificates with potential clients. I post health clearances right on my website. You can check out each breeding dog and see what these certifications look like. If a breeder is unwilling to show you health clearances for their breeding dogs, this is a red flag. I've seen dogs with grade four hip dysplasia who are active and jumping around. You cannot tell simply by looking at a dog whether or not its hips are sound. Ask to see certifications. If a breeder resists, move on.

A responsible breeder will:

- be willing and able to provide you with references;
- be honest with you and have high standards and integrity to provide clients with a quality puppy;
- be willing to work with you even after your pup goes home;

- ask to be kept up-to-date on how the pup is growing and maturing, and about their temperament. (This is how responsible breeders improve their breeding programs. By knowing what my breeding stock produces, I'm better able to pair my dogs appropriately);
- show you health clearances for their breeding dogs;
- provide you with a health guarantee of at least two years;
- vaccinate, microchip and de-worm pups before they go home;
- have some type of adoption form;
- ask you questions about what you are looking for in a dog (This will help the breeder give you the most suitable pup in terms of temperament and coat-type);
- allow clients to visit their kennel, although each one may have different rules (At SwissRridge, I only allow people who have purchased a pup to view the kennel at the time of pickup to reduce the risk of infecting my dogs with diseases like parvo, canine distemper, canine herpes, kennel cough, or canine flu);
- provide you with references from clients, other breeders, veterinarians, etc.
- ask questions to help determine if you will provide a great home to their pups.

Quality breeders will give you support throughout your puppy's life. Remember, when you buy your puppy from a breeder, you are not only buying a pup, you are also purchasing your breeder's advice throughout your dog's life. This can come in handy, as breeders generally have many years of experience in canine nutrition, animal handling, health, and behaviour.

Testing a Breeder

To find out if a breeder is truly knowledgeable, experienced, and well-intentioned, you can ask the following questions:

- Why did you start breeding Bernedoodles?
- How long have you been breeding dogs in general, and Bernedoodles in particular? (You want to know the breeder has

been doing this awhile and plans to continue so that you will have ongoing support)
- What can you tell me about the breed's temperament, health concerns, and coat types?
- What kind of health guarantee do you have? (note: this should cover at least two years)
- Can I see a copy of the contract?
- Can I see health certificates for the parents?
- What is included in the cost of the puppy? (e.g., What vaccines will it have? Is it microchipped? Does it come with a puppy information package?)
- May I see photos of past puppies and speak to their owners?
- What are the parents of the puppy like, in terms of temperament?
- What do you expect the puppies to be like?
- How do you place your pups? Is it "first come first served," or do you help match buyers with the right puppy, based on temperament?
- How do you socialize your pups before they go home?
- Do you provide ongoing support to owners of your dogs?
- Where do your puppies live after they are born, and what do they eat once they are weaned?
- Can I meet the parents prior to pick-up, or on the day of pickup?

Once you have done your due diligence, ask yourself if you trust the breeder, and can envision a long-term relationship with him/her? If you have a bad feeling about the breeder… run!

Did you know… that Bernedoodles do not drool?

Look for the Evidence

Breeders of Bernedoodles should test their breeding stock for hereditary diseases, and share the results with prospective clients.

Bernese Mountain Dogs:
1. Hips (Hip Dysplasia) – Hips are X-rayed and certified by the Orthopaedic Foundation for Animals (OFA) or University of

Pennsylvania Hip Improvement Project (PennHIP) or British Veterinary Association (BVA).

2. Eyes – Eyes are screened by an ophthalmologist and certified by the Canine Eye Registration Foundation (CERF) or OFA.
3. Elbows Dysplasia - Elbows are X-rayed and certified by the OFA.
4. Heart – checked by a veterinarian and certification is sent to OFA.
5. von Willebrand (vWd) Disease – DNA test or blood screen (Checked if parents aren't clear).

Standard Poodles:
1. Hips – as above.
2. Elbows – as above.
3. Eyes – as above.
4. vWd – as above.
5. Sebaceous Adenitis - skin disorder detected via skin biopsy.
6. Heart - as above.

Miniature and Toy Poodles:
1. Hips - for Hip Dysplasia and Legg-Calve-Perthes Disease - OFA, PennHIP or BVA
2. Luxating Patella – kneecaps are checked by a vet and certified by OFA.
3. Eyes – as above.
4. vWD – as above.
5. Sebaceous Adenitis – as above.
6. Elbows – as above.
7. Progressive Retinal Atrophy (PRA) – vet test required if parents haven't been tested.
8. Heart – as above.

* For all sizes of Poodles, tests for thyroid malfunctions are not required, but it's a good precautionary measure.

A Word on Word of Mouth

These days, many breeders have references on their websites. Keep in mind that those references may be old. While that doesn't invalidate them, it's a good idea to balance some recent references with those of long-time owners.

In 2011, I created a Facebook page that allows SwissRidge clients (or prospective clients) to interact with me and with each other. By 2013, it had nearly 1,500 members. It has truly become a hub for dog lovers to share testimonials, advice and photos. My clients actively promote my dogs to newcomers via the Facebook page. They also discuss issues such as grooming, training, and nutrition, among other things. The debates may sometimes be lively, but they are respectful. Everyone is there because they love dogs in general, and my doodles in particular.

Nothing makes me happier than to see my clients raving about their dogs to newcomers. The message carries more weight when it is coming from a happy owner.

I have not had to advertise for more than a decade, and other than the few I donate to charitable organizations each year, I have sold every puppy I've produced.

Owners say...

He really has been a dream come true. Something I love the most about him is that he always seems to be happy. No matter what he is doing his tail is always up and wagging. I have never seen it go between his legs. He is a very happy- go-lucky puppy and it is easy to envision the truly amazing dog he will be. He is the best first dog we could ever have imagined and I could go on forever about how in love we are with him.

I am so thankful that Sadie has such a positive outlook on life. People always comment on what a happy puppy she is... She is such a cuddle-bug and I can't imagine life without her.

He has the perfect mix of Bernese and Poodle qualities. He's very sweet and loves everyone (people and dogs) that he comes across. He cannot imagine a world where someone might not want a kiss on the lips... When he walks the kids to an after school activity, there's a woman who always says 'Here comes the happiest dog in the world.' And he really does attract a lot of attention for his happy-go-lucky demeanor.

Chapter 6

Matchmaker, Matchmaker, Find Me a Dog…

Responsible breeders, large and small, care about the welfare of their dogs. They want the best possible homes for them, so that they are well-loved. Some breeders allow clients to choose their puppy from a litter, often in the order of deposits made.

I used this approach myself when I started out. What I found was that, when confronted with the overwhelming appeal of a litter of puppies, people completely forgot everything they'd learned about selecting the right dog to become part of their lives for 10-15 years. They also became immune to my advice. I'd try to steer them toward the pup I believed best suited their circumstances, but inevitably, they'd decide with their hearts, rather than their heads.

The cute factor usually won out. Sometimes a unique look or color would play into the decision. And one thing I saw all the time was that people would let the puppy "choose them." The pup that galloped over and showered them with kisses was "the one." As you can probably guess, the puppy that's first to approach a stranger tends to be the boldest and most dominant in the litter. While this temperament suits some people, for many, a lower key puppy is a far better fit.

When I finished college and got serious about breeding, I decided to take a new approach. Instead of allowing people to choose their puppy, I would match puppies to prospective owners myself.

This has worked amazingly well. Since implementing my "match-making" system, I can count the number of puppies returned on two hands. And several of those involved changes in family circumstances.

An owner says…Thank you again for pairing us with Ruby. She could not be a better fit for our household and we appreciate everything you did to help throughout the whole process.

The keys to my match-making system are being able to assess a puppy's temperament at a young age, and interpret what type of puppy would best suit an applicant's personality and circumstances.

For the first few weeks of a pup's life, I keep a low profile, allowing them to learn how to be a dog from each other and their mother. At about three weeks of age, I begin handling them more—just enough to get them used to being touched. Because my kennel is large, and I often have multiple litters at the same time, I have several staff that help with this important aspect of puppy care. I make sure to consult with everyone to gather perspectives, as we may see the pups at different times in the day.

A pup's personality starts to show at the age of four to five weeks. Like most breeders, I have an intuitive understanding of puppy temperament from observing so many litters over the years. From the age of 5-8 weeks, in particular, I look at where they rank in their litter, how they interact with their mother, their littermates, and their caregivers. Do they sit back as you come in, or are they the first to come up, jumping at your hand? Are they all over their moms? When they're tumbling around with their littermates, are they always on the bottom or the top? Are they starting the fights, stopping the fights, or just walking away? The answers to these questions tell me a great deal about their personalities.

A puppy that is relentlessly picked on by its littermates, for example, is likely to have a more submissive nature as an adult, regardless of all the socialization and training it might receive. But that personality will be perfect for one of my clients, perhaps a retired person with a quieter lifestyle. The boldest pup in the litter, on the other hand, will be perfect for an athletic young couple that is constantly on the go. Most of the puppies—like most of my clients—rank somewhere in between.

Forty-Nine Days

While I understood much of this intuitively, I wanted a way to formalize and quantify it, so that I could make optimal matches. I decided to develop an assessment based on the Volhard Puppy Aptitude Test, or PAT.

Jack and Wendy Volhard are internationally recognized experts in dog training, health, and nutrition. They believe that if their test is administered at exactly seven weeks—the point at which the dog's neurological development is complete, yet it hasn't learned much about the world—it will accurately predict inherited behavioral tendencies and how the puppy will turn out as an adult.

Although I have adapted the test slightly to suit my needs, like the Volhards, I assess the following in each puppy: attraction to people; comfort with restraint; startle response; acceptance of social dominance by a person; acceptance of dominance while in a position of no control; willingness to do something for you; and degree of sensitivity to touch, sound, and sight.

Each element is scored out of 6, with 1 being the boldest, and 6 being the most timid. A pup that scores mostly in the 1-2 range will be quite dominant and best suited to experienced dog owners who know how to lead. A pup that scores mostly in the 5-6 range will be quite independent and shy, and suit a quiet, structured home.

I average the results across all elements of the test to get an overall ranking for each puppy. Since I began using the test, all of my pups have fallen within the range of about 2.8 to 4.4. The majority fall between 3.2 and 3.8, and I have found pups in that range to be best-suited for my clients. In fact, I work very hard to find the right breeding stock to produce exactly those middle-of-the-road puppies.

Subtle variations in the scores can make all the difference in matching dogs to owners. A puppy that ranked 3 is likely to be significantly more active and dominant as an adult than the one that ranked 4. Of course, I also factor in everything I've learned through close observation of the puppies when making final assessments.

Decision Day

Once I've done the temperament test, I read the adoption forms again and study them carefully. You might be surprised to hear that I have turned down only a few applicants over the years—notably, one couple that got into an argument when they came to collect their puppy (They were not quite on the same page about taking on a dog).

Buying a puppy from me is a significant investment, and most people have put a lot of thought into the decision long before pick-up day arrives. The fact that there is usually a waiting list means it can't be an impulse buy. I am confident that my puppies are going to wonderful homes.

People generally provide a very detailed description of their lifestyle, as well as their preferences, in terms of color, coat type, size, and gender. I look at their family composition, experience with dogs, day-to-day schedule, and activity level. It's important to consider the family as a whole, and see where the dog would fit in. I also need to take into account any allergies and determine the best coat type.

> **An owner says…** *Sadie is an absolutely amazing dog. Sherry did a great job pairing me with the perfect puppy and I fall more in love with her each day. I wanted a dog who was fun and outgoing, but also liked to relax and snuggle. The puppy had to be friendly and love both people and dogs. Sherry gave me exactly what I was looking for.*

The process may not be as fast as people hope. Some dogs that I breed don't conceive when expected. Some produce small litters, or only one gender. Some litters have more tri-color puppies than others. Therefore, applicants who specify that they are set on a tri-colored Bernedoodle may end up waiting awhile. As far as I'm concerned, personality is paramount, so I stress to all my clients that they should keep an open mind when it comes to color. I won't give someone a dog that doesn't suit his or her circumstances simply because it has the right coloring. Sometimes people are faced with the choice between accepting a pup with the right personality and the wrong colour, or waiting until a litter comes along with a pup that meets both their expectations and mine.

An owner says… *Even though I had to wait an extremely long time to get a dog, it was well worth the wait to get the dog of my dreams. Not only is she adorable, but her temperament is perfect for my family.*

By and large, people seem to think it's worth the wait. Since I began matching people to their puppies, I've received daily e-mails from clients who believe they got a dog that suits them perfectly. I always share credit with the owner. While I may have assigned them a pup with strong potential to be their perfect dog, the work they put in after it leaves my care makes a huge difference.

I stand behind my dogs and my decision-making, and if for any reason, someone needs to give up their dog, it always has a home with me. I have successfully re-homed the few dogs that have been returned, sometimes after retraining by my partner, Lucas Mucha. Charleigh is one of those dogs:

We were a bit hesitant to get an older dog but with the training Lucas provided Charleigh it was the best decision we ever made. She is so sweet natured and so well behaved. She loves to work and always wants to please. I know Sherry mentioned that Charleigh arrived back at Swissridge Kennels with some behavioral issues...but I have to say we have not seen any of them. Whatever issues Charleigh had, they were gone. Charleigh quickly and easily fit into our routine and has adjusted so well. She has been with us only 4 months but it seems like she has been with us forever.

Chapter 7

Decisions, Decisions…

Welcoming a puppy into your life should be a joyous event that's long anticipated. For that reason, I never feel terribly guilty about my waiting list for puppies. Impulse buys are best left to beauty products or work-out equipment. So many young dogs end up in shelters, or given away. Not coincidentally, these pups are usually around six months—somewhere between the ages of "adorable" and "needs neutering." The impulse buyer has realized his pup isn't going to exercise and train itself, and it is going to be a significant expense and responsibility for many years. To me, this is heartbreaking. By six months, a pup has bonded with its owner, however neglectful, and the adjustment to a new home won't be easy for anyone.

That's why it's important to do the thinking upfront, and make this major life decision with your head, not your heart.

A Few Hard Truths

Puppies are work. We all know that, in theory, but to understand the full impact, it's a good idea to spend some quality time with one. If you had a dog when you were a child, you need to refresh that experience in your current environment. Even if you had a dog five years ago, you need to take a new look at your circumstances.

Some people consider having a dog to be a warm-up for having a child. It's not a bad comparison; although I have heard many say that life with a newborn baby is easier than life with a puppy. Your newborn won't be chewing the baseboards or biting your hands, for example. On the bright side, a pup grows up a lot faster, and you won't need to save for college tuition.

There's no disputing that the first six to eight months with a puppy are hard work, regardless of your family configuration. There's housebreaking,

71

socialization, basic obedience training, and exercise. Once the initial buzz of having a fluff-ball stare up at you with adoring eyes wears off, you may have moments of wishing you could hit "rewind" and make a different decision. These regrets will become acute during the nipping phase. On the bright side, a well-trained dog becomes the antidote to real work.

Puppies take time. Unless you have an extensive pet support backup system, you can probably kiss most of your hobbies goodbye for the first year of your life with a dog. If you want to raise a good canine citizen, you're going to have to sink much of your free time into that project. The cornerstones are exercise and training and those can't be squeezed into gaps in your busy life. On the bright side, your dog will probably become your favorite hobby.

Puppies are expensive. Again, people know that in theory, but the cost in the first year still comes as a bit of a shock for many—the vet bills, the food, the equipment, the classes, the day care or walker, the kennel when you go on vacation… The list goes on. You might have to give up your daily cappuccino habit to cover the pet insurance. On the bright side, dog walking is good for your blood pressure.

Puppies are a commitment. With a good breeder and a little luck, they're a *long-term* commitment. Spontaneity becomes a thing of the past for most owners. Every decision needs to have a dog factored into it. On the bright side, you'll never be lonely again.

When you're weighing your decision, there's a great tool to help: the puppy adoption form. I designed mine in such a way as to force people to slow down and figure out exactly how they will manage a dog, day in and day out over the long haul. You will have to decide what type of dog works best for you, including the size and activity level. Your analysis can form the basis for budgeting, and get everyone in the family talking about who does what. It really helps if everyone is on board with the decision. Otherwise, the furry new addition can become a source of contention.

Once you've worked through the form, put it aside. Then pet-sit a friend's dog, ideally for a full week, and at a time when you're on your regular schedule. This will test the assumptions you've made in your puppy form.

Did everything work as you expected? If not, how can you modify your plan?

Busy People May Apply

If dogs had a say in the matter, they would no doubt choose to have a couple of stay-at-home pet parents waiting on them hand and foot. This is not a reality for most of us. Someone has to work to bring home the kibble.

Being a solo dog owner, or working long hours doesn't mean you can't or shouldn't have a dog, but it does mean you will have to outsource some of its care. For example, people who work full-time need to make arrangements to get the puppy out during the day. At first, that could mean two or even three puppy visits. Keep in mind that, on average, a puppy can hold its urine for about an hour per age in months, plus one. That means a two-month-old puppy needs to go out every three hours (two hours, plus one). A three-month old puppy needs to go out every four hours (three hours, plus one). Many dog walkers will do two puppy visits for the price of one walk. Your walker will need to understand that the puppy cannot be exposed to other dogs or public places until it is fully vaccinated.

It is a good investment to hire a walker during the workday even when your dog is an adult. Whatever corners you may cut, exercise can't be one of them. If he is walked once during your workday, when you get home from work, your dog will not be ready to explode with pent up energy, and you can spend some quality time on training.

Speaking of training, that too can be outsourced. While you can't avoid working with your dog, you can hire someone else to get you started and cover the basics.

At SwissRidge Kennels, we offer two training programs to help busy owners.

Imprinting

This is a four-week program for pups from my kennel when they are 8-12 weeks old. Puppies get used to the crate, and learn some basic manners and skills, including how to walk on a leash, sit, lie down, and come when called. They are socialized with different objects, dogs, and people, and exposed to various sounds and stimuli. The puppy will be well on its way to being housebroken when it arrives in its new home.

While you will miss out on four weeks of puppy charm, you will also miss the early challenges of getting your puppy adjusted to a crate and trying to socialize it before it's had its shots.

This program is especially helpful for people who live in apartments or condos, and can't just stagger out to the backyard in pajamas at 3 a.m. during those early weeks.

Keep in mind, however, that you'll need to follow the schedule we use during the program when the puppy comes home to ensure you don't lose the benefits of imprinting. Also, you should begin formal obedience classes immediately to reinforce what the pup has already learned, and help entrench yourself as leader.

> **An owner says…** *The puppy was much better than we expected. He actually sits and lays down on command. He seemed to have no trouble transitioning to his new home. He was happy and well adjusted from the minute we picked him up at the airport. He has done excellent in the crate at night – sleeps from 11 – 7 since the first day we got him.*

Basic Obedience

If you work full-time and have other commitments, you may appreciate an intensive training break later on. Pups tend to benefit most from this training after the age of four months, when they have a longer attention span and can learn at a higher level. A four-week training stint will cover all the basics for a well-behaved dog, and address specific problems you may be experiencing.

Doing the Homework

Once you've worked through all the angles, and are fully convinced there's room in your life for a dog for the next decade or more, it's time to do your homework on breeds and breeders.

At this point, I figure it's safe to assume that you've narrowed your choice to a Bernedoodle, and further, that you're seriously considering buying one from me.

If you send me an e-mail to express interest, I will first break the bad news: that you will likely need to wait several months for your Bernedoodle. You might be disappointed at first—because you've gone through this exhaustive decision-making process and you are ready *now*.

Like many people, you may enter a denial phase and convince yourself that there is a way to get a healthy, good-tempered tri-colored Bernedoodle immediately. You might delay sending me your deposit as you investigate every Bernedoodle breeder in North America. It won't take that long, because—as previously discussed—the reputable ones are few and far between.

Meanwhile, you might join the SwissRidge Facebook group to find out from other Bernedoodle owners whether or not the wait is worthwhile. Many owners will tell you it is. What's more, they will post photos of their lovely Bernedoodles and rave about their amazing temperaments. They will answer all your questions, and more. After briefly questioning whether this is a cult, you will most likely fall under the SwissRidge Bernedoodle spell.

You may now enter a phase of bargaining that goes something like this: *What if I settled for a black-and-white Bernedoodle? I could get one of those sooner, and really what's the big deal about a little brown? Will I really care if he's tri-colored in two years? For that matter, will I care if he is actually a SHE? And sure, I wanted a small dog, but a few extra inches and pounds aren't an issue. It's temperament that counts. Right?*

It *is* temperament that counts, along with health. But the exact package it comes in—size, colour, and gender—is up to you. Once you've debated with yourself over what's most important to you, you will come to acceptance, and send in your deposit.

It's official: the wait is on.

What to Expect When You're Expecting… A Puppy

I've heard people say that human pregnancies are nine months long to help you prepare for the complete upheaval of your life. Maybe the same notion applies to dogs. A wait gives you time to plan for the new arrival.

If you haven't owned a dog since you were young, you'll find the environment has changed. I grew up on a farm, where dogs were treated like… well, dogs. Now, most of my clients' dogs are treated like royalty. I'm all for this, of course. But there are almost as many views about dog rearing as there are about child rearing, and people tend to be very committed to their views.

Stop by my Facebook page on any given day and you will find discussions in progress about some big issues. What to feed your dog is a big one: veterinary grade kibble, grain-free, organic, raw… Everyone has an opinion, including me.

Training is another hotly debated subject. Some people lean heavily towards alpha-based training, while others embrace positive-only training. We will focus on training in another chapter, but there are many different philosophies, and the best way to decide on yours is to become informed about the various approaches.

One way to do that is to become part of the conversation on the SwissRidge Facebook page, which will inevitably lead you to do some research. People will gladly recommend their favorite books.

Here are some of mine:

- Sheila Booth and Gottfried Dildei: *Schutzhund Obedience: Training in Drive*
- Jean Donaldson: *Culture Clash*

- Ian Dunbar: *Before and After Getting Your Puppy*
- Jan Fennell: *The Dog Listener*
- Bruce Fogle and Anne B. Wilson: *The Dog's Mind: Understanding Your Dog's Behavior*
- Cesar Millan: *How to Raise the Perfect Puppy*
- Monks of New Skete: *The Art of Raising a Puppy* (Also available in a CD series)
- Clarise Rutherford and David Neil: *How to Raise a Puppy You Can Live With*
- Sarah Wilson and Brian Kilcommons: *Childproofing Your Dog : A Complete Guide to Preparing Your Dog for the Children in Your Life*

Some people might be surprised to see Ian Dunbar and Cesar Millan on the same list, as they are at opposite ends of the spectrum in terms of training philosophies. In my view, there is no "right" way to train dogs, but many wrong ways. Every puppy learns differently, and the more informed you are, the more flexible you will be when you are working with your dog.

Build Your Support System

Most of you will need dog walking and professional training services at some point. As with anything else, the best people are often busy and booked well in advance. Therefore, it's a good idea to check out the resources in your area long before your puppy arrives. Word of mouth is your friend here. Start with dog-owners you know, and if that doesn't pan out, don't hesitate to stop someone on the street who has a well-behaved dog. Most people are thrilled that their dog is being admired—especially when they've worked hard on the dog's training.

When you contact a trainer, ask questions about his or her qualifications and methods. If you like what you hear, sit in on a training session. You might need to do this a few times before you are satisfied. When you know the approximate day of your puppy's arrival, you can book a consultation with the trainer.

Similarly, look into puppy classes, which I recommend beginning after the pup's second round of shots at around 11 weeks.

With a dog walker, again you will want to get recommendations and interview people. The walker must not only be trustworthy and reliable, he or she also needs to be willing to reinforce whatever training style you use so that the puppy is not confused.

Pull Out Your Wallet

I warned you that owning a dog is expensive, and here is where your bank account will take its first big hit. Luckily, you have time to shop around, and do keep in mind that a puppy does not care if it has the best labels. In some cases it makes sense to go high end, in others just get the best deal you can.

Your shopping list:

- a crate with a divider—28-32 inches for a tiny Bernedoodle, 36 inches for a mini and 42-48 for a standard;
- puppy collar—the smallest adjustable puppy collar you can find (I recommend a Volhard or snap collar and sell them on my website);
- leash—six feet long;
- toys and treats—start with Kongs and soft squeaky toys;
- puppy toothbrush and puppy toothpaste;
- food bowls—stainless steel or ceramic, not plastic;
- a dog bed;
- baby gates to contain the pup;
- a cordless dremel to sand your dog's nails;
- grooming tools—slicker curved brush for puppies, and a dematting brush and pin comb for later;
- Bitter Apple spray or other repellant to prevent pups from nipping and chewing;
- Nature's Miracle or similar stain/odor neutralizer;
- poop bags and scoop; and
- a food storage bin.

On the issue of food, you will need to use whatever brand your breeder is feeding the pup to make the transition as seamless as possible. In my case, I ask all my clients to use Royal Canin puppy kibble intended for small, medium or large dogs, as appropriate. That is the food they are weaned onto, and it's easier on their systems if they continue on the same brand.

I also suggest having a can of organic, puréed pumpkin on hand. If a puppy has runny stools from the stress of moving to its new home, a tablespoon of pumpkin in its food can help settle its digestive system.

For supplements, I recommend Ester C to foster healthy bone and cartilage development, as well as Nuvet or Nujoint supplements, which you can order in advance by calling 1-800-474-7044 (Order Code 64857). Dogs love them!

Puppy Proofing

Before your new canine baby arrives, you will have the time and energy to puppy-proof your home thoroughly. Unlike a baby, your pup will be ready to explore its new environment immediately. For a puppy, that means using its nose, paws, and especially teeth. Even if you provide a fine array of chew toys, your pup will want to taste your belongings. It's your job to make them unavailable, or unpalatable through the liberal use of repellent sprays.

Start by thinking like a puppy. Get down on your hands and knees, and poke around your home looking for potential threats. These come in many forms:

- Electrical cords—some dogs aren't deterred by Bitter Apple, so move what you can, or bundle cords with protective covers from an office supply store.
- Cleaning products and other chemicals—move them, or install a child-proof lock.
- Lift curtains and the cords for window blinds out of reach.
- Move wastebaskets or buy covered versions.
- Find a safe place for your cat's litter box—both for the cat's comfort and the pup's health (some dogs love litter treasures!).
- Move all plants out of reach—some are toxic.

- Find a new place for the laundry basket, so that your pup doesn't chew up your favorite T-shirt or pricey lingerie.
- Get into the habit of keeping the toilet lid down and closing the bathroom door, as well as closet doors.
- Pick anything inviting up off the floor, and find a safe, convenient place to put your wallet, keys, phone and chewable electronics.
- Remove rugs from the area that will be your pup's primary play space—bare floor is easier to clean and neutralize odors.
- Start using puppy-friendly products, especially on your floors, as pups can have serious reactions to the chemicals in cleaners and sprays.

Did you know... that Bernedoodles seem to have a "goat" gene? Many of them will ingest socks or other items that will surprise and dismay you. Be extra vigilant in keeping things out of reach, or you may find yourself at the vet's for extraction.

Once you are satisfied that both your pup and your home will be safe, head outside, and yes, get down to puppy level again. Check around your yard and determine if it's safe for your puppy. If your yard is fenced, check for small openings that a puppy could squeeze through. If it's not, consider invisible fencing.

Be prepared to keep your puppy on a leash at all times for the first while, anyway. You could consider a puppy pen, but even then, it is best to supervise a young pup closely. Puppies mouth everything, and most enjoy a good dig. If you value your gardens, I suggest fencing them off. You will also want to make sure any chemicals, such as pesticide and antifreeze, are removed from the yard.

If you have gates, make sure they are self-closing and latching, to keep your pup from investigating the neighbor's yard or running into the street.

Check the perimeter of your house for escape routes, including crawl spaces. Look for hoses and cushions—anything really—that your canine infant may enjoying chewing.

If you have a pond or pool, give some thought to how you will keep your pup safe. You will need to introduce the pup to the water on your terms and show him how to get out. Consider a life jacket as an extra precaution, especially if there will be children and other dogs around. Another big risk is the pool cover. Many puppies have been caught under them and drowned. If your pup does go in your chlorinated pool, rinse them afterwards, as the chemicals are hard on the skin.

Ponds have their own challenges, as they may harbor bacteria or parasites. They should be avoided in the early days, when your puppy's immune system is still very vulnerable.

Delivery Day Looms

Once you've done all you can to prepare, take the advice new puppy owners often give those still waiting: Get some sleep. You're going to need it!

Chapter 8

The Big Day Arrives

Finally! After months of anticipation, it's time for your Bernedoodle pup to come home.

Breeders have different practices, and I can't speak for others. But if you are buying a puppy from me, and live within driving distance, I will invite you to pick up the puppy at a specific time. If possible, I gather several owners from the same litter at once and hold an information session. It gives me a chance to walk people through some puppy basics, and answer questions. It gives new owners a chance to check out each other's pups—and decide theirs is the best. I encourage people who live in the same area to exchange numbers for future play-dates.

In the e-mail invitation, I advise new owners to bring a few things along for the ride: a dog carrier; puppy collar and leash; towels; toys; paper towels in case of accidents; and water and a bowl.

Until my new kennel is operational, new owners will continue to gather in my living room. At this point, people have only seen photos of the puppy I've selected for them and received a brief description of its personality, appearance, and coat type. Their hopes are high that the puppy will be as cute in real life as it is in photos, and as ideal a match for them as I've promised.

The excitement in the room is usually palpable. Some owners have described this meeting as a "blind date." You're about to meet your new long-term companion.

I do my best to ensure you have a positive first impression. Every pup is bathed and fluffed to perfection before you are introduced. One by one, we bring out the puppies and hand them to their new owners.

As I said in my foreword, this truly is a magic moment for me—the moment that makes all the hard work worthwhile. The expressions I see on owners' faces as they receive their new canine friend and family member is priceless.

Between puppy barks and squealing owners, it's usually about 20 minutes before I can get a word in edgewise. During that frenzy, I distribute a package of information and ask everyone to sign my contract. And then, when there's a bit of a lull, I go over of the information that's in the package—the key elements of which are contained in this book.

This session is most helpful for novice dog owners, who haven't endured the puppy stage before. I emphasize the importance of crate training, for example, and discuss my views on vaccines, socialization, obedience training, and puppy care.

I get a puppy volunteer, and demonstrate how to teach a puppy to sit and lie down in exchange for a treat. This is the foundation of the "Nothing in Life is Free" philosophy, which helps to establish owners as pack leaders. I'll go into more detail on this later, but the general idea is that a pup should *earn* all rewards, including, food, play, and attention, by offering something first—such as a "sit." Each pup learns at a different rate, but most pups at age eight-to-ten weeks master sit and down easily.

Many people admit later that they retained very little of the information I conveyed verbally in the introductory puppy session. It's understandable; once your new pup lands in your lap, the excitement on both sides can make it extremely difficult to focus. That's why I suggest bringing along a family member or friend. Between the two of you, you will pick up the important bits. Besides, it's good for your pup to have someone's undivided attention on the way home.

Knowing that I am competing with Bernedoodle pups for your attention, I have a back-up plan: I send home a packet of advice with every pup. And, of course, I am available to answer any follow-up questions you may have. My e-mail inbox is always full, but the volume generally shoots up after a litter goes home. Accept my assurance that no question is too silly to ask. In more than fifteen years of breeding, I have probably heard them all.

Flying High

Many of my clients live too far away to make the drive feasible. Some fly into Toronto, pick up the puppy and take the puppy home on the plane. The benefit to this is that the pup can be with you, in an airline-approved carrier under your seat. If you have time and some travel points to use, it's a great option.

> **An owner says...** *We flew with our pup in a soft crate under a seat with a connecting flight... He slept the entire drive to the airport in the crate...and he slept on both flights.*

For others, it makes more sense—and is usually more cost effective—to have me ship the puppy. Many people are understandably nervous about this. It's hard to believe you can send a tiny pup off in a plane and have it emerge unscathed after many hours, and thousands of miles, later. But it happens all the time. Currently, about half of my puppies take to the skies to join their new families. I offer a flat rate for shipping that includes airfare, a crate, transportation to the airport, the booking fee, and an international health certificate.

I have shipped hundreds of puppies by air since 1998, and have developed an effective strategy. No puppy has ever been injured or lost, and only a few have encountered flight diversions or delays. It's amazing, when you consider how often luggage goes astray. Over the years, however, I have limited the airlines I use to those that accommodate pets the best, and seem to care about the animals' welfare.

No quarantine is required within North America or Europe. It is very simple to take a pup across the border. Customs will stamp paperwork and send you on your way.

SwissRidge Flight Plan

I choose a shipping date when a litter is born and inform people so they can start to plan, but I don't actually book the flight until about five to seven days before the shipping date. Although I try to book direct flights, it depends on the destination, and it's not always possible. Once the flight is booked, I send people an airway bill number, which is required to claim the puppy at the airport. I also forward the time of arrival, the flight number, and an airport phone number to call for directions about the exact location to pick up the puppy.

A week before a litter is to be sent home, I start leaving a plastic carrier in the puppy area, so that they will become familiar, and the pups can wander in and out of it. I also put some toys into the area to take on the scent of the litter and put one in each pup's crate to give comfort in the journey. Owners often tell me that these toys remain their dogs' favorites for ages.

Shipping days start early—usually long before dawn. The pups need to be at the airport three hours before their flight and, as the kennel is a two-hour drive from the airport, I generally set off before five a.m.

At the airport, the puppies are weighed by staff and checked by security before they can be booked in. I attach all documentation to the crate, including my puppy information package, its health record, the microchip information, and the SwissRidge contract.

I check each pup's microchip to make sure it is in the right crate and going to the right person. Then I check again! Despite often shipping multiple pups on the same day, I have never sent the wrong pup to anyone. In fact, my anxiety about controlling every last detail has meant that I only recently accepted help with this routine from someone who is as diligent as I am.

While waiting for the flight, we fill the crates with shredded newspaper, which is both comfortable and absorbent. We brush and fluff the pups in hopes that they will make a great first impression on the other end. Just before the flight, we take the pups to a safe place for a "potty" break, in the hopes that they arrive pristine. It doesn't always work out that way, but we do our best! When the airline is ready for the pups, we put them into the crates with their special toy and hand them over to the staff for loading.

I only ship on planes that have a temperature-controlled animal hold for dogs and cats. Although I can't be sure, I suspect most pups sleep the whole way, because they are tired from the preparations. I never sedate puppies for travel, as there is no one standing by to monitor their reaction to medication. Besides, judging by their speedy and successful adjustment at the other end of their flight, I don't believe they are particularly stressed by the flight. Any eight-week pup leaving its litter and going to a new home experiences some stress—perhaps even more so with a very long drive. But these little creatures are surprisingly adaptable.

Owners say…

Maisy flew into Anchorage, Alaska. I was very nervous waiting for her to come, as she had flown to Minneapolis, transferred to a host family to spend the night, and the next morning flew to Anchorage. I just knew she was going to be traumatized for life! As soon as we got to the pick-up area they handed us her crate. Not a whimper! She came right out of her crate and jumped in my granddaughter's arms. She acted as if she had known us for years. She had not even soiled her crate. We brought her home, she played, and then went to sleep in her crate in our bedroom without so much as a whimper.

Our pup's first day with us started 10 hours, at least, before we got to meet him… He looked at each of us from the back of the crate and then ran and leaped into my six-year-old daughter's waiting arms. It was glorious! He had a nice long pee on his first green lawn. Then another hour-long drive to our home where we had dinner shortly after we arrived. He curled up under my daughter's dining room chair after he finished his meal. Then he slept through the night in the same crate he was shipped in without fussing at all! That was the thing that I could not get over. This baby's world was turned upside down, early that morning. I was truly worried how this traumatic day was going to affect our little guy and couldn't imagine that it wouldn't damage him. How could it not? But it didn't. He just gracefully accepted his new life, literally as if he had always been here with us. Amazing.

Touch Down

I provide owners with a number to call for directions about where to pick up their puppy at the airport. It generally takes the airline about hour to unload pets from the plane. With Air Canada and United, the airlines I use, pet pick-up is usually in the cargo area. Occasionally pet pick-up will be the ticket office. You will want to confirm by calling the contact number I provide.

Make sure you take the following with you to collect your puppy:

- your identification;
- the airway bill number I sent to you with the shipping details;
- enough money to cover the cargo facility's fee of approximately $30;
- paper towels and new bedding, in case the puppy has soiled its crate;
- water and a bowl; and
- a leash and collar in case you need to stop.

When you open the crate to see your puppy, it will be tempting to make a big fuss, but don't. Regardless of the pup's reaction, you will want to be calm and quiet. If the pup is nervous, resist the urge to comfort it. That may seem counter-intuitive, but if you soothe a pup when it is frightened, it reinforces the emotion. From the very first contact, you want to make sure you're demonstrating leadership and rewarding only the right behavior. If you are calm and confident, the puppy will soon realize it is absolutely fine. Keep everything low key, and don't risk overwhelming it with too much attention.

Your puppy will need to stay in its crate at the airport to avoid all risk of disease. If the crate is soiled, someone can hold the puppy during clean up. Then back into the crate it goes until you drive away and can find an area that is unlikely to be frequented by other dogs, or you arrive at home. Only then can you put the puppy on the ground to do his business.

Home at Last

No matter what form the journey took, the arrival of a new puppy is a joyous occasion—something most people only experience a few times in their lives. It's a shame we can't throw a party to celebrate. Instead, it's best to dial back the energy in your home below its usual volume. The puppy's first impression should be that it's in a calm, safe place where decisions are made by taller, wiser creatures.

In short, begin as you want to continue. Keep the fuss to a minimum. Show the puppy the area you've designated as its own. Make sure you have created boundaries, ideally with baby gates, to show the puppy the limits of its territory. You can expand this territory gradually over the coming months until it has greater access to your home.

Introduce the pup to its crate, without closing the door. Offer water and food, but don't be surprised if it doesn't eat very much. Don't force the issue by offering treats, as it sends the wrong message, and also has the potential to cause stomach upset.

Let the pup wander around its safe area and explore, and before long, it will likely fall asleep.

Take that few moments to flip through the puppy package to see what's in there, and pull out the crate training schedule. Study it closely—it's your new bible.

Crate as Safe Haven

It is certainly possible to housebreak a puppy without using a crate, but it takes longer and is more difficult. Some people perceive the crate negatively, but most dogs do not—at least, not after the first week. Almost all puppies will initially protest to being shut up in a crate, but in a shorter time than you can imagine, they begin to see it as their comfortable den. If you play your cards right, the pup will love the crate and retire to it of its own free will.

This will be hard to believe when young Rover is howling like a coyote behind the closed crate door. You will just have to trust me, here. The payoff comes not only in a dog that is speedily housebroken, but in a dog that is able to calm itself and be comfortable on its own. Ultimately, crate training helps to avoid neediness and separation anxiety.

Further, as puppies are notorious chewers, crating protects your home from your dog, and vice versa. In the long term, your dog will be safer and happier, and you will both have more freedom. The crate will even become the pup's "home away from home." So, you must persevere.

If you still have doubts, go at once to the SwissRidge Facebook page and consult with other owners. Their enthusiasm for crate training will convince you. Pay special attention to the reports from people who stopped too early and regretted it.

Best practices:

- Block off part of the crate so that there is enough room for the pup to turn around, and not much more. Extra space may encourage the pup to relieve himself at one end and sleep comfortably at the other.
- Use towels in the crate unless the puppy chews soft bedding. If so, you can try a firmer crate pads, or if necessary, go bare.
- If the puppy does soil the crate, clean thoroughly to eliminate the scent.
- Remove your puppy's collar and leash before placing him in the crate, in case it gets caught in the wires.

Cover your Ears

While I don't crate puppies before they are eight weeks of age, I do place one in the puppy area for them to explore, so it will not be a foreign object to your pup. When you get home, let the puppy wander around its designated area and check out its crate. Place a toy that has the scent of its mother and littermates in the crate, or perhaps some wood shavings from the kennel zipped up in a small pillowcase. Add a few tasty treats to the crate—all with a goal of tempting the pup to go in and make himself at home. Only when the pup is comfortable in the crate should you close the door.

When it realizes that it is confined, the puppy may communicate a serious protest via whining, yipping or even outright howling. Your job is to hold firm. Despite all evidence to the contrary, the pup is not being tortured. Stay in sight, but don't react to the theatrics in any way. Absolutely no reassurance allowed!

Put on noise cancelling headphones if you must, or turn on some soothing music, and prepare to wait the puppy out. Eventually, it will stop complaining and you can open the door. When it does, pick up the pup and take it outside immediately. Say "Go potty," or choose your own phrase, and when it does its business, reward it with praise and a tasty treat. Then enjoy some playtime with an empty pup.

If the pup does not go potty within 10 minutes of being outside, put it back in its crate and try again in 10 minutes. Puppies will soon get the idea that without going potty, they forfeit playtime.

Rinse and repeat. This is how your life will look for awhile, with the uncrated gaps getting longer and longer as the pup gains control. At first, you are the one being trained, and ultimately, the pup will be trained as well.

> **An owner says…** *That crate training schedule really kept me on track. I needed the structure. Plus, my dog was trained in record time.*

Puppy Crate Training Schedule

Eight-Twelve Week Old Puppies

6:00 a.m. – Go out

6:10-6:30 a.m. – Free period in one room

6:30 a.m. – Food and water in crate for 20 minutes; remove food and water

7:00 a.m. – Go out

7:15 a.m. – Free period in one room

7:45 a.m. – Back in crate

10:30 a.m. – Go out; back in crate

12:30 a.m. – Go out; food and water in crate for 20 minutes; remove food and water.

12:45 a.m. – Free period in one room

1:15 p.m. – Back in crate

3:00 p.m. – Go out

5:00 p.m. – Food and water in crate for 20 minutes; remove food and water

5:30 p.m. – Go out

6:15 pm. – Back in crate

8:00 p.m. – Water in crate (No water after this point)

8:15 p.m. – Go out

8:30 p.m. – Free period in one room

9:00 p.m. – Back in crate

11:00 p.m. – Go out; back in crate

3:00 a.m. – Go out; back in crate

Three-Six Month Old Puppies

7:00 a.m. – Go out

7:10 – 7:30 a.m. – Free period in one room

7:30 a.m. – Food and water in crate for 20 minutes; remove food and water

8:00 a.m. – Go out

8:15 a.m. – Free period in one room

8:45 a.m. – Back in crate

12:30 p.m. – Go out. Food and water in crate for 20 minutes. Remove food and water.

12:45 p.m. – Free period in one room

1:15 p.m. – Back in crate

5:00 p.m. – Food and water in crate for 20 minutes; remove food and water

5:30 p.m. – Go out

6:15 p.m. – Back in crate

8:00 p.m. – Water (in crate) – go out

8:15 p.m. – Free period in one room

9:00 p.m. – Back in crate

11:00 p.m. – Go out; crate overnight

Six- 12 Month Old Puppies

7:00 a.m. – Go out

7:15 – 8:00 a.m. – Free period in one room

8:00 a.m. – Food and water

8:30 a.m.– Go out

9:30 a.m. – Back in crate

12:30 p.m. – Water and food

12:45 p.m. – Go out

1:45 p.m. – Back in crate

6:00 p.m. Food and water

6:30 p.m. – Go out

7:30 p.m. – Back in crate

11:00 p.m. – Go out; crate overnight

Housebroken Adult Dogs

7:00 a.m. – Go out

8:00 a.m. – Food. Unlimited daytime water supply

12:30 p.m. – Go out

6:00 p.m. – Go out

11:00 p.m. – Go out. Remove water for night

This is a general framework for housebreaking using a crate. Some people will need to adapt to suit the dog's habits. For example, some dogs relieve themselves immediately after eating; others wait half an hour or longer. Once you learn how long nature needs to take its course, adapt the schedule accordingly. Just be consistent, and ensure that every family member adheres to the schedule as well.

The puppy should only be out of the crate when you are able to watch him closely. As he matures and becomes more trustworthy, you can give him longer periods of freedom until he only needs to be confined in the crate when you go out. This will come with time.

Always take the puppy outside:

- As soon as he wakes up in the morning.
- After every meal and drink of water.
- After he awakens from a nap.
- Before any extra freedom period.
- After unusual excitement and/or long play periods.
- The last thing at night.

You may be going out with your puppy 10 times a day during the first week he is home, but once you work out a routine, six times a day will usually suffice.

The First Night

Hopefully you took my earlier advice and built up your sleep bank, because the first week with your pup may not be completely peaceful. He is, after all, adjusting to an entirely new life, with no warm littermates surrounding him.

At bedtime, put your pup in his crate with his special toy, possibly a warm water bottle wrapped in a towel or a snuggle puppy. You may want to play soft music in the background.

Owners say:

I found that sitting next to the crate and singing to him has made him settle down and fall asleep and then he seems to be fine after he's put back in the middle of the night as long as he can hear I'm nearby. It's hard to hear them missing their dog pile! Oh, and I put a big stuffy dog toy in there with him to give him something to snuggle up to.

I took off the shirt I'd been wearing all day and put it in the crate with the puppy to comfort her.

We used a stuffed sound machine—the kind you purchase for a newborn's crib. It worked like a charm. We also had her crate right next to our bed.

She actually howled in her crate for the first three days. We just kept up with the schedule and she hasn't made a peep since. Another thing that helped was that we moved her crate into the living room/kitchen area so that she could be in the middle of the action for most of the day.

We actually moved her crate from the living room into the master bedroom and she was able to see us go to bed. We took her on a longer walk right before bed. We also threw on some music as we were getting ready for bed and after the first three nights, she's been a champ ever since. She knows when light music comes on, its bedtime!

We covered the crate, leaving the front and back open for air flow. This made it seem more "den like."

I played a "clock tick-tocker" beside her crate and sat near her crate until she calmed down and fell asleep.

Although I don't generally recommend having puppies in the bedroom, many people find it easier for the pup to adjust that way. If you choose to keep the pup's crate in your bedroom, at least in the first few days, it will likely calm down more quickly and awaken you less. Over the next week, you could gradually move the crate further away, until it is situated where you would like it to be.

If the pup whines in the night, it's important to let it try to calm itself down. Too much soothing talk will lead to a longer adjustment period.

It might be a rough few nights, but most people report that the puppy is sleeping six to eight hours after the first couple of weeks.

Keep in mind that while general rules apply, each pup is different and develops at its own pace. Some will potty train like champs, and others might take a little longer. These are smart dogs and they will all get there in time.

If you need some moral support in the tough early days, head back to the SwissRidge Facebook group, where someone will have encountered any challenge you face. Don't hesitate to ask for advice.

An owner says: *The SwissRidge Facebook page is a godsend.*

And of course, anyone who buys one of my pups is free to contact me at any time. Never worry that your question is silly. If it concerns you, it concerns me.

Chapter 9

The Honeymoon Period

As you stare, bleary-eyed, at the crate training schedule on Day Two of your new life with your Bernedoodle puppy, you may not recognize this as a honeymoon period. But it is. The pup is likely still subdued after his transition into your home, and he's too small to get into a whole lot of trouble, especially since you've thoroughly puppy-proofed in advance. All you really need to do, between pots of coffee, is feed and water the pup, play with him, and take him outside periodically. Easy, right?

Of course, you'll need to fend off the many people who are begging to see the new addition to your family. It's better at this point to keep the environment as calm as possible. Delay your dog-loving friends as nicely as you can, though, because in a week or so you're really going to need them as you ramp up socialization.

At this point, the only person I recommend seeing is your vet. In fact, my contract stipulates that you must get a general check-up within three days of arriving home. I suggest getting it done immediately, to put your mind at rest that your Bernedoodle is as perfect as it looks.

When you get to the vet clinic, carry your pup inside, and don't set it on the floor. Naturally, veterinary offices see a lot of sick animals, and your little one does not yet have a strong enough immune system to fight off infection. Make sure the examination table is wiped down with disinfectant before placing your pup on it.

Your vet will examine the pup from top to bottom, checking for things like an improper bite, a heart murmur and an umbilical hernia. You should collect a sample of your dog's morning stool and take it along with you. Despite my strict de-worming program, it's possible that some pups will have a parasite. These cases are rare and can be easily treated. Dogs can pick up parasites anywhere—puddles, grass, ponds, soil or feces left behind by other animals—you will want to discuss with your vet a future prevention program.

The initial puppy exam is a great time to ask your vet about any concerns. For example, your pup may not be eating well, or may have loose stool, and your vet will likely reassure you this is natural, and due to the stress of moving to its new home. Ask your vet about routine care, such as nail trimming and ear cleaning.

While you are at the clinic, ask the vet to sign the pet insurance form I included in your puppy pack. When you get home, you can follow the link from my website to register for 30 days of free pet insurance from Trupanion (trial number BRAFF515A). The offer is valid for 24 hours after the first vet visit.

And since we are taking care of business, make sure you also register your puppy's microchip information, and send me a copy of your signed contract, if you have not done so already.

Vaccines and Socialization

You will also want to discuss the schedule for vaccines, and how much socialization the vet recommends before the pup is fully immunized. It used to be common practice to seclude pups until the last round of shots, at the age of 16 weeks. Research has shown, however, that the most critical time to socialize a dog is *before* 16 weeks of age. Therefore, most vets will say that after the second round of vaccines, it is not only acceptable but advisable to sign up for a puppy socialization class. Any reputable training facility will keep clean premises and request proof of immunization for dogs participating in classes. (If they don't, keep looking!) The benefit to the pup will outweigh the risks.

Puppy vaccines protect against parvovirus, distemper and hepatitis, and finally, rabies. (Your vet may recommend other vaccinations.) The first set of vaccines is given at seven or eight weeks of age, while the pup is still with the breeder. Your vet will administer two more sets of vaccines at three- to four-week intervals.

Here are some general guidelines:

First set of vaccines: Puppies must stay at your house. Don't take them on roads, sidewalks or to parks—essentially anywhere another, potentially ill, dog may have visited. You may allow other dogs that you know are fully vaccinated and healthy into your home or yard to play with your pup.

Second set of vaccines: Puppies can attend puppy socialization class after getting their second round of shots. Continue to avoid the side of the road and parks.

Third set of vaccines: Your dog can be considered fully inoculated about a week after its last set of vaccines. At that point, it is safe to take your pup most places, including dog parks.

The Leadership Project

So, you're working the crate training schedule like a pro and you're confident your dog is healthy. Now it's time to begin a project that will continue throughout your Bernedoodle's life: providing leadership.

Perhaps the best way to establish your dog's place in the family is simply to introduce the "Nothing in Life is Free," or NILF, program. This positive-based training approach, endorsed by the Humane Society, essentially requires a dog to earn everything it wants. The things dogs want most are food, treats, toys, and attention—resources that you control.

You can get started with the NILF program by teaching your pup some simple commands: sit, lie down, come, and watch me. Reward him each time with lots of praise and a treat. Once your dog has mastered a few commands, you can begin to request that he perform one of those commands before you give him something he wants. He will quickly grasp that you are in control of All Good Things.

As examples, tell your pup to sit before you place his food bowl on the floor, or lie down before you throw a toy. Later, when he masters more complex commands, you will make him sit and wait at the door before you open it and step outside.

At the same time, you must be careful to avoid unconsciously rewarding the wrong things. If your pup nudges your hand, you may automatically start to pet him, without realizing you've just been told what to do by your dog.

If you are sure that your dog understands a command, wait until he delivers before you give him what he wants. If he refuses to perform the command, simply hold out. Eventually he will have to obey to get what he wants.

The beauty of the "Nothing in Life is Free" program is that you are establishing yourself as a leader in a positive, non-confrontational way.

Basic Commands:

Sit: Hold a treat at head level and move it back across the pup's skull, towards his ears, and say, "Sit." You can use your other hand to tuck the puppy's bum into a sit.

Down: Lure the puppy down by tucking a treat between its front paws on the ground and saying "Down." Give the treat only when the pup is fully down.

Stand: Bring a treat up to the puppy's head level and draw it forward, saying "Stand." Once he is standing, give the puppy the treat.

Now you have the components of a "puppy push-up." Go through the routine of sit- down-stand again and again, and switch up the order.

Watch me: Get the pup to focus on a treat. Say "watch me," and put the treat close to the bridge of your nose. When he looks at the treat, say "yes," and give him the treat. This will teach your puppy to focus on you and watch for your next command. When you have the pup's eyes, you have its attention.

Come: Start working on this essential command immediately. Kneel, waggling a toy or a treat, and call, "come." Praise, reward, repeat. Gradually work up to more distracting situations, using a long leash in the yard, and eventually a park. Until your pup has a completely reliable recall, you must keep him leashed so that you can follow through on the command.

Leave it: Hold your dog's favourite treat in the palm of one hand. Show the puppy the treat and say, "Leave it"—once, and in a firm voice. When the puppy goes for the treat, close your hand. The puppy will lick and paw at your hand. Wait till the puppy looks away and then offer the treat in your opposite hand, and say, "Take it." With practice, you will be able to leave a treat in your open palm and the pup will ignore it until you give the okay. Once your puppy is reliable with this command, practice outside, and ultimately in parks. "Leave it" will become a multi-purpose command to deter your pup from eating garbage, chasing squirrels, approaching aggressive dogs or even nipping.

Drop it: If your pup already has an object you want it to release, such as a sock, offer a higher value treat in exchange, and say, "Drop it." Practice exchanges with objects of increasing value. For example, if your pup has a bully stick, you may need to offer a piece of chicken or hot dog to make the exchange worthwhile for him. If the pup believes you always have better things to offer, it will prevent guarding behaviors when you need to take something away.

> **Did you know…** That you can use some of your pup's regular kibble allotment for rewards throughout the day? For learning new commands, however, you will likely have more success with "high value" treats, like bits of chicken—whatever your dog loves most! Try heating meat for a few seconds to release the scent and motivate your dog to do its best for you. Most pups will do anything for bits of steak, but be aware that it may be too rich and cause stomach upsets or loose stools.

Staying One Step Ahead of Your Bernedoodle

As we've already seen, Bernedoodles can inherit both the smarts of the Poodle and the obstinacy of the Bernese Mountain Dog. You are going to have to start strong and stay strong when it comes to setting the rules.

Creating boundaries for your puppy—both literal and figurative—can help establish your leadership and build a respectful relationship. Dogs are hierarchical creatures, and if you don't take your place at the top, they'll assume the leadership role is up for grabs.

Unless you want to be reporting to your Bernedoodle, here are some guidelines:

- Be calm, focused, fair, and consistent.
- Ignore behaviors you don't want to see, and reward the ones you *do* want to see.
- Get a solid foundation in obedience to learn how to work with your dog.
- Move forward in a situation only if your dog is calm, whether it's approaching a person, another dog, or greeting someone in your home.
- Pass through doorways and other openings first. You lead; the dog follows.
- Close off certain areas of the house to the dog, and allow access only when you choose.
- Keep the furniture for the humans in the family—especially the bed.
- Periodically take over some of the places your dog typically claims. For example, move his crate, or block his favorite nap location.
- Eat before your dog does. Then, have the dog do a down-stay to wait for his own dinner. Pick up his bowl after a set amount of time. Avoid free feeding.
- Control the busiest areas in the house. Don't let the dog block main entrances or hallways. Use baby gates to make your point.
- Provide affection on your terms, and only when the dog is calm and obedient. If he's nudging you to be patted, or barking for attention, withhold attention until he "earns" it by obeying a command.
- Focus on petting the head, neck and shoulders, and use firm, dominant strokes.
- Don't allow your dog to place a paw on your body, and stay off the floor when you are playing. Your dog should not be on top of you.

- Control access to toys. Make the dog obey a command before you offer one, and collect toys when playtime is over.
- Avoid tug of war games and roughhousing, where your dog can get overexcited and dominant.
- Ignore the dog when you first come into the house until the dog is calm.
- Work on obedience daily.
- Brush your dog frequently and do handling exercises.
- Create simple rules that everyone in the family can follow, and make sure everyone enforces them.
- Make sure you can follow through on any command, and don't give a command if you can't.

I know some of these may sound tough, but it's important not spoil your puppy. That will set you up for a power struggle, and believe me when I say that it is much easier to start out the right way than to remedy a more serious issue later. You want to build a relationship with your puppy from the beginning based on love and mutual respect.

Building the Bond

In adopting the boundaries outlined above, you may start to worry that your pup won't like you. Believe it or not, the firmer your boundaries, the happier your dog will be. It will understand exactly what you want and know how to deliver. A dog needs to see its owner as someone to look up to, and rely on. This tends to come more from training than affection. It's fine to give your dog affection if it is calm and behaving well. But remember a strong bond grows not only from hugs and kisses, but also from respect and trust.

To some degree, bonding with your puppy is natural and inevitable, but it is also possible to enhance that bond with some effort. The more bonded your dog is to you, the more he will want to listen, learn, and please you. The better trained he is, the more you can do together, thereby intensifying the bond even further. It comes full circle!

A dog's willingness and capacity to bond can vary with breed. Some breeds attach very strongly to one person, and exclude others within the family. Needless to say, with my goal of breeding fun, family dogs, I prefer dogs that are a little more egalitarian. Purebred Bernese Mountain Dogs tend to form intense attachments, but adding a good dose of Poodle genes generally produces a more flexible dog in the Bernedoodle. In fact, many Bernedoodles are so outgoing that they work the family, and even the neighborhood, like politicians.

> **An owner says…** *Alfie is a social butterfly. Showing up to the annual neighbourhood Canada Day barbeque is like arriving with a celebrity. All you hear is "Hey Alfie! Hi Alfie, good to see you! Looking good, Alfie!"*

I've come to know both Poodles and Berners inside out, and bringing the two breeds together in the Bernedoodle seems to create an alchemy that produces a dog with a very special capacity to bond.

> **An owner says…** *It's not just bonding deeper… It's more that they want more from me/us than my Bernese Mountain Dogs wanted. They want more love, more interaction, more touching, more eye contact, more training (yes, they totally love training!). They seem to connect with us on more levels than previous dogs did. It is so gratifying to see how interested they are in you, and you can't help but fall in love with them.*

The good news is that Bernedoodles tend to spread the love around to the entire family. While your pup may attach most strongly to its primary caregiver, and be more responsive to that person's commands, generally Bernedoodles will form different kinds of relationships with other members of the family that are equally deep. For example, if someone spends more time playing with the dog, the two will have a relationship based more on fun and affection, than on leadership and respect. Most owners find that Bernedoodles are a bottomless pit of love, and say that the dog is happiest when its whole "pack" is together.

> **An owner says…** *I feel as though he is very bonded to both of us, but in different ways. He follows me around more but he knows that he can roughhouse with my boyfriend and not me. He always wants to be where we both are.*

Every dog is an individual. Some will be more affectionate, and some will be more independent. Their personality usually mellows as they mature. By breeding easygoing parents with the right personality, I tend to produce dogs that fall into the middle ground—not so affectionate and dependant on your that they become anxiety-ridden if you leave, and not so independent that they prefer to have a room to themselves.

Although older dogs can and do bond strongly to their new owners, in general, the strongest bond forms when you start working with a young puppy, especially between the ages of 10-16 weeks.

In fact, when we keep young pups for the Imprinting Program, we make a concerted effort NOT to bond with the puppies. We do this by making sure a number of different people handle them and work with them, which serves a complementary goal of making sure they are well-socialized. When these pups go home, they are primed to form a bond with their real families.

Most of the time—but not always—the person who spends the most time with the dog and does the most work will have the strongest bond.

An owner says... *She follows me everywhere, lying right at my feet when I'm at the table, washing the dishes or on the couch. Yes, she LOVES everyone, and appropriately gives them wet greetings and affection, but she always returns quickly to me, lavishing her devotion on "Mom." I think it's a time, care, fun, training, personality, all-in-one package thing.*

I recommend starting to work on the bond as soon as your puppy arrives. In addition to the bonding exercise I've outlined below, this can be as simple as calmly petting and holding the dog, as well as brushing it. As your pup grows, spending lots of time with him, and working together on training, will establish a strong relationship. Exploring the world on leashed walks will connect your dog to you ever more strongly. That is how you will ultimately be able to let your dog *off* leash in open areas. He will be so attached that he has no desire to go far without you.

> **An owner says…** *You need to LOVE them. They are really receptive to lots of love and attention… Sounds crazy I know, but they are people, with feelings, stuck in furry bodies.*

Just the same, it's important to foster some independence as you will not be with your dog constantly. Although Bernedoodles are not particularly prone to separation anxiety, it's a good idea to get any pup used to being on its own early. So, when your puppy is still small, park it in its crate with a chew toy and leave for a couple of hours. Increase the length of your absences gradually as the dog matures. When you think your dog is ready to be left uncrated, again start incrementally. If you come back and your dog is dozing and your furniture is intact, you've done your job perfectly: the dog is attached and yet fine on its own.

Bonding Exercise

I have found this bonding exercise to be excellent for building trust with a dog, and establishing leadership. It also allows you to do a physical examination every day, and catch any problems early, like small lumps or an ear infection. Your pup will get used to being handled from head to toe, which will be a huge help later, when you are grooming the dog or administering medication. All family members should work through this exercise. You will find a video demonstration of it at http://www.swissridgegoldendoodles.com/bondingexercise.html

Start by kneeling behind the puppy. Tuck him into a sitting position by placing your hand under his bum and your other hand on his chest. Then gently lift his front paws and place him in a "down" position,

---

without applying pressure to his joints.

Hold your puppy down with one hand and use the other to do the exercise. If your puppy struggles at any point during the exercise, growl at him as his mother might, and put him back into position. You may need to repeat several times at the beginning, but eventually he will calm right down and become very relaxed.

Work through the following steps, telling him what you are doing:

Gently massage his shoulders, saying "shoulders."
Massage the front legs, saying, "legs."
Touch in between the webs of all toes.
Touch each nail, one by one.
Massage the head. (The pup should be very relaxed by this point)
Look into each eye and pull down the eyelid, making sure everything looks normal.
Lift up the lip, and run a finger toothbrush along his teeth.
Lift up each ear, make sure they are clean, and pluck out a few hairs each day.
Massage the chest.
Place the puppy on his left side. Check under the stomach, the pads of his feet, his armpits and under the tail. In unneutered males, check the testicles for lumps.
Take the front legs in one hand, and the back legs in the other, and gently flip the puppy to its other side. Examine everything, as you did in the previous step.

Once you have completed all the steps, say "release," and praise your puppy.

I recommend doing this exercise every day for the first year, and twice a week thereafter. It will give you a structured session to examine your dog for ticks and anomalies.

Puppies and Children

I am a huge proponent of family pets. Being raised on a working farm, I was surrounded by a veritable menagerie, from dogs to goats. The animals became my favorite playmates as I grew. As a child, I ran a small petting farm and offered pony rides to visitors—and we all know where my fondness for animals eventually led.

While most children won't develop a career from caring for family pets, experts attest that they will likely gain better impulse control and self-esteem. Caring for pets can instil nurturing behaviors, and help children develop empathy. It can also reduce anxiety and ward off loneliness. Plus, owning pets can often motivate a child to get outside and exercise.

While I believe owning pets can teach children responsibility, a dog is a *family* responsibility. If you get a puppy with the expectation that your child will do most of the hard labor, you are likely doomed to disappointment. But your child will be happier, even if you are the one getting all the exercise.

Bernedoodles are a great choice for children. In fact, they are bred to be family dogs. The Bernese Mountain Dog, in particular, is a breed that is patient and loving with children.

An owner says… *From the moment Ellie [the dog] met Sam [the baby] we knew they'd be best friends. Even though Ellie has a very sweet gentle personality we still had reservations about how she would be with a baby since Ellie was only 7 months old herself when Sam was born. Having Sam in our family has really brought out Ellie's maternal side. When he cries she gets to him almost as fast as we do to make sure he's OK, sometimes bringing him whatever toy she was playing with. When we put the baby down Ellie gives him a thorough sniffing and a few gentle licks. We were concerned about the licking until we found out it's just her way of welcoming the baby into her pack. Her favorite place to sleep used to be on the bed as close to her people as she could get. Now she positions herself to watch over the entire family. We feel very lucky to have such a good dog.*

A Bernedoodle may come wired to fit into your family, but that doesn't mean it will all be smooth sailing. And when the nipping phase hits, don't be surprised if your kids suggest returning the pup!

Here are a few tips for weathering the adjustment:

- Get everyone in the family involved. Even a young child can have a responsibility for a minor aspect of the pup's care.
- Enlist the kids' help to keep all small toys out of the pup's reach (especially things like Lego).
- Encourage the kids to be gentle and to stay calm, as quick movements can over-excite a puppy.
- Make sure the puppy gets some space, ideally in his crate.
- Allow children to hold a young pup only while they are sitting, in case they drop it.
- Involve your children with training from day one—they can teach puppy push-ups and make the puppy work for treats.
- Let your children add a few treats to the pup's bowl so that he will not guard his food, and use the exchange program so that the pup doesn't become possessive of toys.
- Prepare children for the nipping phase and arm them with a strategy. A light six-foot floor leash will allow anyone in the family to give the pup a time out when needed.
- If the pup is acting up and all else fails, children should leave the room and return only when the puppy is relaxed. Remember that depriving a pup of attention is a severe punishment indeed!

An owner says… *Pups and kids are a great and dangerous combination at the same time. The greatness comes from the need to adjust to the other, respect and treat each other properly. The dangerous aspect is that they are really **both** pups, so they have to be supervised to be sure that everyone plays by the rules. If kids are rough, they get a time out. If pup is nippy, puppy gets time out. It is also important for puppy to realize that kids are their 'Alphas,' so kids need to be integrated into the training of dogs through the simplest of tasks.*

From the very start, it's important that your puppy be gently handled by many children, so that the pup will understand limits and develop patience. If boundaries are set, this can become the most profound and loving bond.

A Biting Machine

All puppies nip, growl, and jump up on people. This is completely natural to them, and they will continue to do so until they learn that their human family is different from their littermates. It's crucial to teach a puppy that nipping is unacceptable. Helping them learn to withhold the bite is challenging, and it takes time. Here are some tips to reduce the pain:

- When a puppy nips your hand, redirect him with a chew toy.
- Use Bitter Apple Spray or tiger balm on your hands.
- If your puppy nips you, try growling at him, as his mother would. Or try yipping, as a littermate would. Stop all play and leave the room. Or remove the puppy from the situation.
- Counteract bad behaviour by requesting good behavior. If he nips or jumps, make him sit and then give him a treat.
- Teach the puppy the "leave it" command as soon as possible, and use it.
- Keep a Volhard collar and a light, six-foot-long leash on your puppy so that you can address bad behavior. If your pup nips or growls, give him a five-minute time out by tying him to a door handle. (Never in the crate, as it is his "safe place" and should never be used as punishment.) When a dog is in a time out, ignore him completely.
- If necessary, leave the room. Don't make a big deal about it, and don't flail your arms. Either tie a long leash to a door knob, or step over a baby gate so the puppy can't follow you. This will teach the pup that you start and stop all games.
- Stay calm so that the pup will mirror the energy you project. If you are excited, he will get hyper.
- Give your puppy lots of appropriate exercise to discharge that crazy puppy energy.

There will be a point in the biting phase where you think, "This is never going to end," but miraculously, it does. I promise that you will get through this truly annoying stage and find a sweet dog on the other side.

> *An owner says... I just want to tell you again how much we LOVE our pup. He is amazing, funny, sweet and so, so loving. It's really incredible how he knows "who" belongs to him. He is definitely most bonded to me in many ways, but whenever my son is around it is clear the pup's focus shifts to him. They are both so young, and haven't QUITE figured out the best way to play with one another without one of them—or both of*

them—getting into trouble, but there has never any malicious aggression from either one towards the other, and there have been no grudges or developing fears. It really is so special to watch this relationship in particular unfold.

Chapter 10

Becoming a Bernedoodle, in Seven Stages

Like all breeds, Bernedoodles go through seven developmental stages. These are loose divisions based on my general observations. Every dog will progress at its own pace. It's important to note that large dogs, including Standard Bernedoodles, grow and mature more slowly than smaller ones. While the first eight weeks are pretty standard for all pups, after that there will be variance.

Dependence (Birth to One Month)

When pups are born, their ears and eyes are closed, but their noses are already operational. They can recognize their mother and littermates by smell, and this sense becomes keenly important to them throughout their lives. At this stage, a puppy can't regulate its own body temperature, and must be kept warm to survive. Puppies have limited immune systems, and depend on antibodies from their mother's milk to protect them. By the time a pup is three weeks old, it can see and hear, is starting to walk and testing out its bark. At the end of this stage, puppies can urinate and defecate without their mother's help.

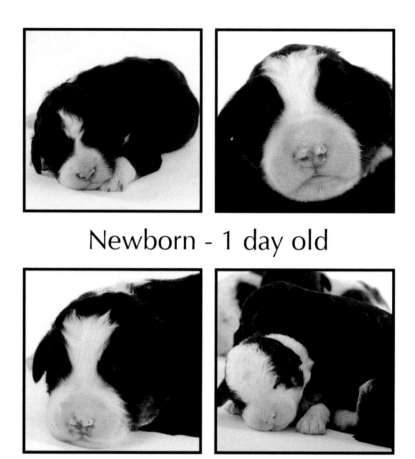

Newborn - 1 day old

Learning to be a Dog (One to Two Months)

At this stage, a puppy begins to realize it is a dog. This is widely considered to be the most critical social development period of a pup's life, as he interacts with his littermates. It's critical that the litter remains with its mother at this point to learn proper dog etiquette. Otherwise, the pups may be at a deficit with other dogs for the rest of their lives. In particular, they learn about bite inhibition—how hard they can chomp down on their littermates without hurting them. In fact, when they are not sleeping or eating, the pups are usually roughhousing. Their mother mostly lets the pups work it out themselves, occasionally stepping in with a correction. This teaches them how to exist in a hierarchical pack. Pups start eating soft kibble around four weeks. Their mother spends less and less time with them, and by the age of eight weeks, wants very little to do with them.

Handling puppies during this stage and exposing them to different sights and sounds will increase their confidence. I take this early socialization very seriously, and make sure puppies are handled extensively throughout the day by different people. I believe this is one the main reasons my clients are so happy with their SwissRidge dogs. A good dog starts with a good puppy that's been properly socialized by the breeder.

I've witnessed a thousand pups go through this stage, and it never ceases to amaze me how much they change in a few short weeks.

Launched (Two to Three Months)

Most puppies join their new families at this stage. They are primed to bond and eager to explore, still more or less the proverbial blank slate. It's probably the easiest time to teach your puppy, as he's small enough to control and willingly accepts you as leader. He is also primed to learn new skills. What he learns now will stay with him for life, so make the most of the opportunity. Expose puppies to new situations, providing there is a low risk of infection. Begin some training and focus on socialization to equip the puppy to handle change as it grows.

While every puppy is different, most enter a fear period at some point during this stage. Try to avoid any extreme experiences during the fear period (e.g., fireworks), as these can be exaggerated ten-fold in the pup's mind. However, if the pup does get frightened, project a calm air of "business as usual." Comforting a frightened pup reinforces the emotion. Instead, walk the pup through the situation, and praise him on the other side for being brave. This fear period may be very subtle and last only a few days. But if you see it, don't be concerned as it does pass.

Nipping and roughhousing increase for all breeds of puppies toward the end of this stage—so much so that you might start to wonder if there's a bit of Tasmanian devil in their genes.

It's a Good Thing He's Cute (Four to Six Months)

This stage is one many owners would like to skip! Most pups become brats at this point, and there is no way around it. Your pup isn't a baby any longer, but he isn't ready to be reasonable, either. He will waver between overconfidence and timidity, keeping you on your toes.

For mini and tiny Bernedoodles, the super-growth spurt will slow down by the end of this stage, and their appetites will taper off. Standard Bernedoodles will continue steady growth, eating you out of house and home.

Your pup will lose its baby teeth and break in its permanent teeth on anything in its path—hands, feet, clothing and furniture.

Clear, consistent leadership will save your sanity—and your belongings. Go back to the tips in the previous chapter and make sure you're following them. For example, redirect the pup from biting inappropriate things to toys and chew sticks. Set boundaries and stick to them. Reinforce that the pup's place is below that of other family members. Above all, have patience.

On bad days, you will vow never, ever to get another puppy.

By the time this stage passes, your pup will be much taller, and its permanent coat will be coming in.

Testing Limits (Six to Eight Months)

This stage is the doggie equivalent to the "teen" years. Your puppy will readily learn commands and what you expect of him, but will continue to test your limits. It is very important during this period to follow through on commands. In fact, you should only issue a command if you know you *can* follow through.

The Bernese Mountain Dog genes may show themselves at this stage in stubborn behavior, and without consistent leadership, you will both become frustrated. Your long and lanky teen will become more independent and wander further afield. It will also reach sexual maturity. Many people neuter and spay their pups at around six months. I recommend waiting till eight months or more, particularly for standard Bernedoodles, so that they can achieve full, proportionate growth. This is something to discuss with your vet, and you will also need to take into account your dog's behavior. If you start to notice dominance issues, spay or neuter right away. Some males can become a handful at this point.

Your dog may also experience a second fear period at this stage, or early in the next one. This fear period may be more noticeable, but the same techniques for managing it apply.

Almost There (Nine to Twelve Months)

During this period, smaller Bernedoodles will reach full growth, and become more mature. A standard Bernedoodle still has a way to go; your pup should stop growing at around 18 months, but won't fully mature until two years of age. Standards will still be in the adolescent stage, and will continue to push your limits.

But for most dogs, this is a great time of life. They are playful and exuberant, yet learning all the things they need to become full-fledged dogs. As they become more seasoned and experienced, you can gradually increase the scope of their freedom and activities.

Destination: Adulthood (One year and up)

You may start to have doubts about whether your dog will *ever* settle down, but somewhere in this stage, it will. In fact, sometimes it seems to happen almost overnight: one day your dog is still challenging everything you say, and the next recognition will dawn in his eyes. All your hard work training will start to pay dividends, as maturity and knowledge come together. You will heave a big sigh of relief.

And then you may wonder if you should start over with a second dog.

The Wonders of Exercise

Most people have heard the expression "a tired dog is a good dog." For the most part, that is true. Your dog will thrive with the right amount and quality of exercise. Mature dogs need consistent, daily exercise to keep them happy and healthy. If they don't have that outlet, they will find ways to use their energy that you will not appreciate—such as chewing, or barking. Here's another expression: "A bored dog is a bad dog."

That said, it's important to scale up the exercise as a puppy matures. When your Bernedoodle first comes home, he will need several short bouts of exercise each day. This is best accomplished by taking the pup for three or four 15 minute walks, and by playing. Chasing a ball in the yard will burn off a lot of puppy energy.

If you cannot be around to provide this exercise at intervals throughout the day, I recommend hiring a walker to take the dog out and play with it. Similarly, you will want to get into a formal training program early on and continue for the dog's first year. Old dogs can learn new tricks, but it is so much easier to start early. Make the first year count.

Too much, Too Soon

While a tired dog is a good dog, an *over*tired dog can be unmanageable, and at risk of injury. Like toddlers, they often don't know when to stop, so you will need to moderate them.

Walking is considered to be "forced exercise," and the repetition can take a toll on a pup's growing skeleton, especially on asphalt. For this reason, some experts recommend a five-minute rule: a pup can walk five minutes on a leash for each month of age on one outing. That means at three months, the puppy would walk on a leash for 15 minutes, and at six months, for half an hour.

Depending on the dog's size, its skeleton may not fully mature, and the growth plates fuse, until it is over 18 months of age. Before the growth plates close, excessive exercise, or the wrong kind exercise, can cause stress to the skeleton, and ultimately result in permanent damage, including elbow and hip dysplasia and joint problems. The damage is unlikely to show up until later in a dog's life, at which time exercise may become painful.

Here are my general exercise guidelines for Bernedoodle puppies:

- Keep walks to three or four per day, of no more than 15 minutes each.
- Walk and play on grass, where possible.
- Limit climbing and jumping—carry your pup up and down the stairs.
- Wait until the dog is physically mature before taking on vigorous activities such as jogging or agility classes. For miniature Bernedoodles, that means about a year, and for standards, 18 months to two years.

Probably the single best energy-draining exercise for Bernedoodles is fetch, played on grass. It allows for bursts of energy that will tire your dog out in a way leash walks can't, without harming their joints. It also allows you to practice basic commands with your dog. Fifteen minutes of fetch, along with a couple of leash walks, should see your dog through to a healthy old age.

Most puppies love to roughhouse with other dogs, and it's a great outlet if they have a well-matched, fully vaccinated companion. In fact, play is the best vehicle for learning, whether it's with other dogs, or humans. But all dog-on-dog play must be supervised, as it can quickly get out of hand. Puppies can be injured or scared, and develop inappropriate behaviors. If you see that your dog is stressed, getting picked on, or picking on other dogs, remove him from the situation immediately. Give him a time out to calm down before allowing him to re-enter the situation. If you can't do the same with the other dogs, end the play session. A bully can affect your dog's personality and behaviour. Try to keep every experience with your puppy a positive one.

Teaching your dog basic commands will give you control over your dog when it is roughhousing. You need to be able to call your dog out of uncontrolled situations, and tell him to "leave it." When your pup comes at your call in the middle of play, you know you are on the right track to a well-behaved dog. Be sure to reward him for it.

The Right Fuel

Puppies grow very rapidly in their first year and need to be fed a good quality puppy food. These days, there are as many brands and types of food as there are breeds of dogs, and everyone has an opinion—including me!

After trying more than 20 brands of food, I settled on Royal Canin, and have found great success with it. My adult dogs are healthy and energetic, and have thick, shiny coats. I believe a dog's coat quality, level of energy, and general health stem from the quality of its food. I wean my pups onto Royal Canin puppy food, and send them off to their new homes in great condition.

When your pup gets home, feed them the following amounts *three times per day*:

Tiny Bernedoodle – one-third cup of Royal Canin mini puppy dry food
Mini-Berndoodle – one-half cup of Royal Canin medium puppy dry food
Standard Bernedoodle – one cup of Royal Canin large breed puppy food

If you can't get Royal Canin in your area or want to try a different brand, I have heard good reports about Acana, Taste of the Wild and Performatrin Ultra.

I add a number of supplements to my dogs' food, which I will outline in Chapter 14.

I advise against feeding your pup an all-stages food. Puppies need to be fed a puppy food, specifically targeted to its eventual size. Keep your tiny and mini pups on puppy food until they are a year old. Standards can stay on puppy food until they are 18 months of age.

Like many breeds, Bernedoodles can have food allergies. If your dog has dry, itchy skin, or gets a lot of ear infections, you may want to try changing its food. In this situation, I usually suggest avoiding dog foods that contain chicken. A good place to start is a dog food that combines a single protein with a single carbohydrate. Salmon and sweet potato formula dog foods often work wonders for a dog with allergies.

Too Busy to Eat

In their early days in their new homes, puppies often show little interest in their food. Their appetite will pick up in time, but you can try to kick-start the process.

Owners say:

Sometimes hand-feeding them a few kibbles will get them to start eating the rest on their own.

Try adding some warm water and see if that helps.

Don't make a fuss. Just set the food down and find something quiet to do nearby. If mealtime becomes loaded with anxiety, your pup will sense your anxiety and feel anxious, too. As long as he is still acting playful, you can be pretty sure that the lack of eating is not due to illness.

A Word about the Runs

Most dogs experience loose stools on occasion that can last a day, a week or longer.

Puppies are particularly prone to diarrhea because they have sensitive stomachs and their digestive system needs time to mature. It is not unusual to see blood or mucous in loose stool because of irritation in the lining of the intestine. This will stop once the diarrhea is under control.

If your Bernedoodle puppy gets the runs, here is my advice:

- Take him to the vet for examination, to make sure he doesn't have a virus or parasites. Take a stool sample with you.
- Avoid all treats until the stool firms up.
- Add a tablespoon of pure pumpkin purée to his kibble for a few days.
- If the diarrhea is severe, feed the pup only hamburger and rice, and gradually reintroduce kibble.
- Switch kibble to a gastro formula from the vet until the pup's system settles down, and then gradually introduce regular puppy kibble.
- Add a probiotic, such as FortiFlora (available from the vet), or plain Kiefer (available from the grocery store).
- Add canine digestive enzymes, on the advice of your vet.
- Try a food designed for puppies with sensitive stomachs, such as Taste of the Wild's Pacific Stream puppy formula.
- Avoid vaccinations if your pup is showing signs of digestive upset.
- Keep the puppy in a quiet and stress-free environment.

Finally, watch your puppy like a hawk to make sure it is not eating garbage, poop, grass, dirt, or stones. Puppies will eat things that will leave you shaking your head. The only solution is vigilance and mastery of the "leave it" and "drop it" commands.

Chapter 11

The Winning Combination

I breed healthy, even-tempered dogs that come to you with the genetic makeup to be wonderful companions. But where my work essentially ends, yours begins. It's through diligent training that your dog's promise will come to fruition.

I've spoken about training in various places in this book, but the subject warrants an entire chapter. Training forms the foundation of a long and happy relationship with your dog. Shelters are full of dogs that never got the training they need.

I never have to go far for training advice, because I have daily access to an expert, Lucas Mucha, the resident trainer at SwissRidge Kennels. Lucas is my partner in life, and all things dog.

When I met Lucas, my standards for canine etiquette were not particularly high. I kept my breeding dogs on a large property in a rural location. They didn't need to be perfectly trained. And while I took some of them to obedience classes, there were not enough hours in the day to work closely with all of them.

I've had the benefit of Lucas' wisdom for many years now, and my standards for canine etiquette are still not particularly high, to be honest. I always say that I want "good dogs." By that, I mean that they need to listen and obey basic commands. They come when called, walk on a leash, and treat other dogs and us with respect.

I believe most of my dogs have the intelligence and temperament to be beautifully trained therapy dogs. But it isn't going to happen. Time spent on advanced training would be time taken from my work.

Like all of us, I compromise. My dogs only need to be good enough for me. Likewise, your dogs need to meet *your* standards. Some of you will want a perfectly trained dog that practically reads your mind. Others will be satisfied with a "good dog."

Achieving even "good dog" status takes work, though. Left to their own devices, as too many are, dogs will jump all over people, counter surf, mark their territory inside and out, dig up your garden, chase squirrels, bark incessantly, and chew up whatever smells interesting. That is a dog's idea of the good life.

Your job is to teach them that what *you* want is really what *they* want. Pleasing you must become the Prime Directive. When you are happy and can trust your dog, they will have more fun and freedom.

It doesn't happen overnight, but with patience and persistence, it does happen.

> **An Owner says...** *Now that I have invested time, energy, and a few dollars into training and understanding what my dogs are trying to communicate to me, their temperaments are unbelievable. I spent some time being very frustrated at the behaviour of my pups, but after understanding why the older dog was acting out at me, when the younger dog was driving him crazy, I was able to become the leader of my pack and control their temperament.*

A Born Trainer

Some people have a gift for working with animals. It's more than just a passion. Few people love dogs as much as I do, yet I am not a natural trainer. I have to work at it, just as you will.

Luckily, life threw someone into my path who does have that gift. Thanks to him, the dogs in our large "pack" are well balanced. Breeders can sometimes have trouble with so many high-spirited, unneutered dogs in one place. Our dogs exercise in groups and they all get along. That is due in no small part to Lucas' leadership. He sets the tone.

I suspect most of the dogs prefer him to me, but I figure it's the price I have to pay for hooking up with someone who isn't just good with dogs, but *great.*

The signs were there very early in our relationship, when I took Lucas along on a visit to a horse farm. The owner warned me that his dog was very suspicious of strangers, so I wasn't surprised when it bolted away from me. We went to check out the horses, and 20 minutes later, I looked around to find Lucas on the barn floor, cuddling the dog, as well as two barn cats. The farm owner was stunned. As far as he knew, no one had ever touched the cats. Yet they adored Lucas.

That's when I realized Lucas had a very special gift with animals, and I have seen it manifest time and time again. During our time together, he has rescued and rehabilitated many extremely aggressive dogs. One of those dogs bit me, trapped me in the house, and menaced my staff. But from the start, Lucas could roll around on the floor with him. Eventually, he trained that dog out of its aggression and now everyone can handle him.

I used to doubt that he could rehabilitate some very sad cases—dogs that other trainers gave up on—but he has proven me wrong every time. He seems to know exactly what to do and how to act to gain a dog's trust. In six years, I've seen him work with more than a hundred dogs, and there has never been one he has not been able to train.

In the course of my life with dogs, I have met and worked with many skilled trainers, but I have never seen anyone that has such a profound connection to animals.

Some may think I am biased—he is my boyfriend, after all—but the results speak for themselves.

> **An owner says...** *Lucas quietly observed our family's interaction with our pup. He was able to identify the cause of our pup's mannerisms and then translated into "human terms" what we needed to do to obtain the desired behaviors. Each member of the family took the lead and had Lucas work with them on the do's and don't's. It was the "why" we need to implement these changes that had impact on the kids – it meant they*

would be able to walk their puppy (instead him walking them!). It meant no more mouthing when playing. It meant having a puppy that respected, instead of challenged them!

Teaming Up

When we met, Lucas was working as a dog trainer with a security company, and owned one dog. I mentioned that I bred dogs, but was deliberately vague on the specifics. I knew my lifestyle wasn't going to suit many men, but fate must have intervened when our paths crossed.

Still, Lucas was somewhat shocked to find himself surrounded by about 20 dogs on his first visit to my home two months later. He quickly adapted however, and not only embraced, but revelled in my dog-centered life.

Initially, he mainly worked with what I would call "tough" dogs, and I wondered what he would think of my passion for sweet-natured, family dogs. Happily, Lucas loves all dogs, of every size and every breed. He truly does not discriminate.

Over time, as my clients began asking me for more advice about training, it became a service we offered at SwissRidge.

In addition to the four-week puppy Imprinting program, we also offer the intensive in-board basic obedience course, in which dogs over age four months learn to be "good dogs." They leave here with excellent recall and leash skills, and everything else you need to coexist peacefully. For those who truly want a perfect dog, we offer advanced training. And for dogs with serious behavioral issues, Lucas might just be a lifesaver.

The Training Continuum

There are many approaches to training, and the subject can be quite polarizing. Those who adhere to a strictly positive, treat-oriented training approach often scorn any kind of correction other than a time-out. Those who embrace a strict "alpha" approach see treat-oriented owners as walking Pez dispensers.

We believe that many paths can lead to a good dog. Instead of adopting a single approach to training, we treat dogs as individuals and tailor methods to suit each dog's personality. Some dogs are highly motivated by treats, some by praise, and some by toys or games.

There is no question that food-oriented dogs are the easiest to train, especially when they are very young. When pups are not interested in working for food, you need to get creative. There is always something a dog really wants, and through trial and error you can find it. With these dogs, it gets easier as they mature and become more motivated by toys and playtime.

Once you know how to motivate your dog, it is a matter of practice and patience. Bernedoodles, like most dogs, love learning, and if you keep your sessions short, positive and frequent, you will quickly see remarkable gains.

Keep in mind that every puppy is different, so you need to be flexible. In our four-week imprinting course, we spend the same amount of time with each puppy. At the end of the program, some pups are walking well on a leash, and have nailed "sit," "down" and "come" like tiny champs. These pups really want to work and please their owners.

Other pups in the same program may not come wired with the same drive to work, and may not be treat-focused, so it takes them a little longer to pick up the basics.

In surveying my clients, I invited them to ask Lucas questions, and they covered everything from basics to trouble-shooting. You'll find his answers to the most common questions below.

What is the best part of your job?

Rehabilitating dogs that are labelled a lost cause and successfully placing them into new homes is the best part of my job. Those are the times that I absolutely love what I do.

What is your general approach to training?

I believe that a willing student is the best student, and that all obedience should be conflict-free. It is critical to keep obedience positive.

My approach varies from dog to dog. I would not approach a dog who is dominant the same way I'd approach a submissive dog. However, I always try to achieve results with *helping* the dog to change, rather than by forcing it to change through dominance or compulsion. My goal is to keep the dog's trust. I do believe there are instances where correction is necessary.

What are the best habits owners can keep with their dogs?

Never baby your dog. Walk your dog daily on lead. Practice obedience. Do the bonding exercise in Sherry's hand-out package daily. Reinforce behaviours that are positive and ignore behaviours that are negative. Use time-outs to guide a dog into making the right decision.

What's the secret of being a pack leader? Are we all capable of becoming one?

Anyone can be a good dog owner. I believe a relationship with a dog should be based on mutual respect and trust. A dog will push boundaries, and it's your ability to keep your boundaries intact that will make you a good dog owner. Depending on your personality and ability to set limits, you may need a more submissive dog that does not test the boundaries as often. Think about your own personality when you are working with a breeder to choose a puppy. A good breeder will know which pup suits you best.

What should an owner's first priorities be in terms of training when a new puppy comes home?

Crate training, bonding, socialization, and basic obedience that is conducted in a positive manner.

How can owners enrich their puppy's development to ensure a well-mannered and content puppy?

Socializing in many, varied situations with positive outcomes will help shape the puppy into a social, happy dog.

What are some common mistakes dog owners make without realizing they are making them?

It's a mistake to comfort a dog that is in a bad state of mind, because this only nurtures the behaviour. Other mistakes include not socializing the dog enough with other people or dogs, and petting a puppy while it is jumping up on you, which creates a dog that jumps later on. A dog will keep behaviours that were rewarded, so if you allow a young puppy to jump at your knees, chances are it will still do the same thing when it has put on 60 pounds.

It's also a mistake to abuse the "come" command. Use "come" only when you *really* want the dog to come, and be sure to offer a high reward for obeying. You don't want the dog to start tuning you out.

Repeating a command endlessly is another common mistake. e.g., sit, *sit*, SIT! Issue your command once, and wait for the pup to obey. Depending on the stage of training, you may need to show the pup what to do again by luring it with a treat into a sitting position or tucking it physically into a sit. Remember that you must always follow through on commands.

How do I take leadership on a walk, so my dog doesn't think it's walking me?

As you put on the leash, set the mood for your walk. Have the dog sit, and when you're ready to go, have him sit-wait at the door as you exit first. Letting the dog pull you out of your house means he has control from the start. Focus on keeping a slack leash while walking. (See reference to "loose leash" walking" later in this chapter)

How can you ensure that what you're teaching in a session "sticks"?

Keep things positive with high reward. High rewards will reinforce something in the dog's mind much more effectively. Remember, your reinforcement has to compete in the real world with things like chasing squirrels and playing with other dogs. So you need to really build up what you reinforce. I always tell people to think of the dog's brain like a scale: if a dog wants to chase a squirrel but you tell it to come, the higher reward will always win. However, if you have reinforced the "come" command tirelessly, the dog will choose to come because of the history of a high reward factor.

Do you have special discipline "tricks" up your sleeve?

I find I can use body language quite effectively. I think people need to be more aware of how they are using their body language and make sure it's communicating what they really intend. For example, when you are walking your dog on leash, make sure your shoulders are back and your arms are relaxed. If you walk with calm confidence, your dog will sense your mood and be calm, too. If you tense up when you see another dog, for example, your dog will feel the change in your energy and may become tense, nervous or aggressive.

Bernedoodles

What do people need to know about training a Bernedoodle?

Bernedoodles are very smart dogs with a stubborn streak. The same training principles apply as to any other dog, but you might need a bit more patience and practice.

Every Bernedoodle is different, however. It is really important to have your breeder match you to a puppy that suits you.

Do you find major differences between Bernese Mountain Dogs, Poodles and Bernedoodles, in terms of training?

A dog is a dog and each has a unique personality.

Bernese Mountain Dogs are sensitive, yet strong willed. Poodles are very intelligent and learn new things quickly. Both are dogs that want to please their owners.

When training a Poodle, I find you can move quickly as they learn very fast. It might take the Bernese Mountain Dog a little longer to learn the same things.

With the Bernedoodle, the training will depend on which traits they've taken from the Bernese or the Poodle. The best approach also depends on the particular Bernedoodle's personality. You will need to study your dog and decide what works for him or her.

An owner says... *He is extremely stubborn and I have to stay on top of him constantly or he would run all over me. Mostly he just tries to turn everything into a game.*

If a Bernedoodle inherits the sensitivity and the strong will from the Bernese Mountain Dog, what approach would you recommend?

I would use a method that does not give a dog the chance to be strong willed. This means using a high reward to keep the dog focused and willing to perform the task. Find something that your dog really loves, whether it be treats, a toy, or affection. He has to love it enough to be willing to work for it.

If you have the dog's eyes and attention, and it really wants the food or toy, it will work for that and it is less likely to show its stubborn side.

With a dog that is sensitive, it's critical to keep training positive.

Multi-Dog Owners

In general, do you think dogs are happier if there's a second dog in the family?

Yes. Dogs love having another canine companion. They are pack animals by nature. If you have the time to spend training both dogs, it's a great idea.

Is Bernedoodle a good choice for a second dog in your household?

Bernedoodles are social, fun-loving dogs that are great with people, dogs, and other animals. They will make a great addition to your "pack."

What combination tends to work best, in terms of gender?

A male and female usually works best, as they don't compete for the same things in life. However any combination can work as long as there is a good pack dynamic.

How far apart should you get your dogs?

Make sure you have complete control of your first dog before you decide to get another one. Your first dog can then help a lot in training your second dog.

What is the best way to introduce a second dog into your family?

You want to introduce your first dog and your new puppy on neutral ground. So take your first dog off its territory and introduce it to the puppy. Let them play for awhile, and then walk them home together.

Ask your breeder to send you a toy with the puppy's scent on it in advance, and introduce that to your first dog before bringing home your new puppy.

Most dogs love companionship and introducing a new puppy is not usually a problem. However, if your dog does not like other dogs, you might want to think twice about getting a second one. The last thing you want is a new puppy to be ruined by a dog that is aggressive or territorial towards it.

> **An owner says...** *I found that what really bonded our [dogs] has been time together away from us. We send them to day care together every week or two. I think being on neutral ground, without fighting for our attention, has helped them bond and become their own little 'pack', still with us as the leaders. They really watch out for each other now.*

How can an owner of multiple dogs keep peace in the ranks?

In most instances dogs will work things out on their own. However, you should intervene if the situation is starting to turn aggressive. The aggressor would be separated into a time-out away from the family and the other dog.

How do I stop my dogs from being jealous when I give one attention and not the other?

The best way to fix a behaviour is to help your dog come to a realization and *want* to change its mind. If the dog is placed in a time-out for butting in or being jealous it will come to the realization that its behaviour caused the time-out. So the dog will try to adopt the behaviour that keeps it in the situation.

What do you do if your dogs fight with each other?

Dog fights can be dangerous. Your dog will be in a different frame of mind and you might be bitten if you get involved. If your dogs are fighting, I recommend contacting a professional. A trainer can help you figure out why the dogs are fighting, and what you need to work on within your pack to prevent the behaviour.

What advice would you give to someone who wants to get a third dog?

The most important thing is to look for a puppy that will fit into the pack dynamic. If you have a dominant dog already, you don't want to get another dominant puppy as they will end up fighting for a high rank in the pack. You will need to work with your breeder to find a dog with the right temperament that will complement your pack.

Then you will need to work on training your new puppy, just like you did with your first two dogs, so that it will be a well-integrated part of your family.

If you have three dogs, I suggest neutering them before they have a chance to reach maturity, as it makes handling them much easier.

> **An owner says…** *Having three dogs is interesting as there is definitely more dog psychology required than for two dogs. For someone who was not really on top of these things, it would be chaos.*

How do you handle dominance issues in a "pack"?

There will always be one dominant dog in a pack. You can't fight nature. Dogs will quarrel over rank until they know where they fit in a pack. A well balanced pack means every dog knows where it fits and they are not fighting for a position. The problem comes when you have a pack without structure. If the dogs are fighting, consult a professional trainer to help you through this.

Having total control of your pack will eliminate dominance issues, as well. Follow the advice in this book about bonding and setting up boundaries. Dogs need to understand that you control everything in their life.

> **An owner says…** *It certainly wasn't the 'love at first sight, let's cuddle together' that I was hoping for and it probably took a good six months for them to really bond. The pup just loved the older dog to bits, but the feeling wasn't mutual. They are fully connected now and play together, cuddle together. But they also have moments where they each want the same toy/bone/parent… just like human siblings I guess. I've learned that the key is to be sure that each dog knows they aren't the leader, the humans are. It is a constant work-in-progress on our part.*

Trouble-shooting

What problems do people bring to you most often? How do you fix them?

Dominance issues are the most common problem I see. I fix them by setting rules for the dog and doing obedience training. Once you establish with your dog a relationship based on mutual respect and trust, your dog will respect you and this should fix dominance issues. Your dog will stop wanting to take control of situations and start looking to you to take control. There will no longer be a power struggle.

What kinds of training challenges frustrate you most?

The thing that frustrates me is when I put a lot of work into training a dog, and return it with a set of instructions, but the owners don't follow them. What takes weeks to instil in the dog can be lost in just a few days if the owners go back to their old ways. It's very disappointing to see a well-trained dog revert to its previous inappropriate behaviors. Everyone is happier when a dog is well-trained—including the dog.

What sorts of problems would ring alarm bells with you?

I would recommend getting a professional trainer on board when a dog bites a person or another dog, or when owners feel they've lost control of the dog and nothing they try is helping.

How do you feel about dog parks?

I don't like dog parks because many people who use them do not have full control over their dog. You don't want to put your dog in a situation that will compromise its temperament or life experience. Also your dog can pick up bad habits from poorly trained dogs.

I prefer off-leash hikes as a way to burn energy, but you must have total control over your dog before you do this. Your dog needs to be listening to your commands at all times under distraction.

And in my view, *nothing* replaces the need to walk a dog on lead.

How do I socialize a big puppy with smaller ones, when she doesn't realize her size?

If a puppy is getting rambunctious, remove it from the situation and put it in a time out. Then reintroduce and repeat as necessary until the puppy realizes what action is causing it to be taken out of play time.

My dog gets too aggressive when he wants to play with us, or with another dog we see while walking. He will jump, nip at our hands and bark. What do we do?

If your dog does this during a walk, turn around and go the other way. Once the dog is calm, walk towards the stimulus again. Keep repeating the process until your dog stops the unwanted behaviour.

If the dog is doing this at home or in a dog park, remove the dog from the situation and only allow him back into play time when he is completely calm. Setting rules and following them at all times will fix these power struggles.

Another strategy is redirecting your dog's attention with a treat or a toy. Give your dog a command to do something to earn the treat, and take its attention off the stimulus.

My dog only responds to "come" if he feels like it, or knows I have a treat. How do I get him to come every time, even in new environments?

As with every other command, the key is practice. You need to continually reinforce your obedience with the dog.

If your dog will not come 100 per cent of the time when you call it, keep a lead on him. This way, when you tell your dog to come and it doesn't, you can reel it in with the lead and follow through with the command every time. Starting in your yard, put the dog on a 15-foot leash and tell it to come. Then progress to practicing in a park under distraction.

My dog gets very excited when he meets new people. How do I keep him calm?

Keep the dog on a leash, and step on the leash so that the dog cannot jump up. Give the "sit" command and tell the new people to ignore the dog completely. Only when the dog is calm may new people greet the dog. If the dog performs unwanted behavior, walk away. Wait till the dog is calm, and try again.

How to get her to be calm at the door when somebody comes over?

Once you have taught and reinforced the sit and stay commands, you can put the dog in a sit-stay when someone knocks at the door.

Keep a mat by the door and send your dog to the mat. (With a new puppy that hasn't learned its commands, a family member may have to hold the pup on the mat with a leash and collar.)

Once guests have come inside and settled, you can release the dog from the sit-stay. Guests should ignore the dog unless the dog is calm.

When this happens often enough, the dog will learn the behaviour and automatically go into a sit and stay when someone comes to the door. Dogs are creatures of habit.

My dog is very nervous around people (or other animals, loud noises). What can I do to help?

Slowly expose your dog to stimuli. Once the dog is comfortable with the amount of the stimulus, slowly increase it. Make sure to positively reinforce any curiosity or confident behaviour the dog displays with a treat or praise.

It is important to expose your dog to lots of stimuli early on, so it will learn to accept new situations without anxiety. Remember to ignore nervous behavior and reward confident behavior.

How do I stop my dog from:

Nipping

As the puppy's teeth make contact with your skin, yelp and walk away. Repeat this process. You can also use toys to redirect the nipping. Try your dog's favourite toy so that the attention stays on the toy rather than your hand.

Chewing

Most of the time dogs chew out of boredom. Lack of exercise or anxiety can also be culprits.

Use bitter apple or other repellants on the things your dog is not allowed to chew. Redirect your puppy to objects it can chew, such as toys, bully sticks, or antlers.

Pulling on the leash

Train the dog with "loose leash" walking. Start with a slack leash. Simply say, "this way," and walk your dog in one direction. As soon as your dog passes you and puts tension on the leash, change direction and once again say, "this way." Your dog will learn that you will walk with him towards a direction if the leash is loose, but that he will not get there by pulling.

Barking

If your dog is barking too much in the house or yard, try using a muzzle. As soon as your dog starts barking, put the muzzle on. After five minutes take it off. Repeat as long as the dog continues to bark.

You can also control barking by teaching the "bark" command, followed by the "quiet" command. Start by triggering a bark, by getting someone to knock on the door or ring the doorbell, for example. When the dog barks, reinforce with a treat. Repeat, fading the trigger and replacing it with a hand gesture or the word, "speak." Do not reinforce the dog for barking *without* your cue. The dog needs to learn that not all barking is rewarded. Once you have mastered the "bark" command, get someone to knock on the door to trigger barking. Say "Quiet," or put a finger to mouth and say "Shhhh." Then reward the post-bark silence. Make sure to keep the tone in this training positive.

Digging

Try placing dog poop on its favorite digging site to deter it.

You can also build a small sandbox in your backyard and bury a chew bone in it. Bring your dog to the sandbox and let it find the hidden bone. If he tries digging elsewhere, keep bringing him back to the sandbox until he understands that's the only place it's permitted.

Jumping up on people

Start with a "sit" command. Step on the leash so that the dog cannot jump. If the dog breaks this command, turn around and walk away. Return and try again. If the dog sits, let the person praise him and reward the dog with a treat. Every time the dog presents a negative behaviour, such as whining, crying, jumping, or lunging, turn around and walk away. The point is to get the dog to sit at every encounter with people and reinforce this.

Eating poop

In general, the best way to prevent a dog from eating anything it shouldn't is to teach the "leave it" command.

Some puppies start eating poop in an attempt to clean their living area, such as the crate, similar to what their mom would do. Cleaning up right away after your puppy poops will help prevent this habit from taking hold. Never scold your puppy for pooping in the house, as it may try to "hide the evidence" the next time by eating it.

As they mature, they should develop a distaste for it. You can speed up the process by sprinkling hot sauce on the feces.

If poop eating becomes a problem, make sure to rule out any health issues that might be affecting the dog's absorption of nutrients, and causing it to eat inappropriate things.

Growling at my kids and being too rough

Remove the dog from the situation and give him a time-out from the family, out of view. (Don't use the crate for this.) Reintroduce the puppy to the situation after it has calmed down. This will control the level of play and teach your puppy what is acceptable.

Being aggressive on leash towards other dogs

Teach the "watch me" command, and reinforce daily to build it up. Once the command is firmly entrenched, tell the dog "watch me" when another dog is in sight. Start further away from the stimulus and slowly move closer and closer.

If you have the dog's eyes you have control.

Barking crazily when the doorbell rings

Teach the "quiet" and "bark" commands. Then expose your dog to the stimulus yourself.

Ring the doorbell and reward the dog when it is quiet, and ignore the dog if it barks. Do this as much as possible to get the dog used to the sound and reinforce quiet behaviour.

Submissive urination

If your dog is prone to submissive urination, it's essential to be very calm with the dog, especially at greeting. If you are excitable, it will cause the dog to get so excited that it will urinate.

Leave the house in a calm manner and return in a calm manner—it's all business as usual. If you let your dog get excited when you arrive or leave, its anxiety level will increase and potentially lead to separation anxiety or submissive urinations.

Socialize the dog with as many people as possible in a calm, positive manner. Progress only as quickly as the dog's comfort level indicates.

Submissive urination normally improves as the dog matures.

Beyond the Basics

It's impossible to cover every possible training challenge in one chapter—or even an entire book—so we'll stop here. Lucas is always available to help, whether or not your dog comes from SwissRidge Kennels. Check the training page on my website to learn more.

Chapter 12

The Upside is the Downside

One of the Bernedoodle's biggest assets is that it does not shed, or sheds very minimally. Most of the time, you will be very happy about that. There won't be fur balls drifting across your dark hardwood floors, and you can throw away your lint brush. But to be honest, some of the time and effort you might have spent cleaning up after a dog that sheds will need to be redirected into maintaining your Bernedoodle's coat.

The amount of maintenance required varies from dog to dog, but generally speaking, the more "poodle in the doodle," the more work it will be to keep mats at bay. Curly coats mat more easily. But all Bernedoodles will need regular coat care. Some do fine with a thorough brushing once a week, but most benefit from more frequent attention. Mats are no fun for either you or the dog, and you will end up needing a very short cut if you don't stay on top of this. A shorter clip will require far less maintenance.

My advice, quite simply, is to start brushing your puppy as soon as it arrives. Your puppy will be small, easy to handle, and more or less accepting of this new experience. I'm not saying he'll like it. Most of them don't at the beginning. Using a puppy brush with soft bristles will help. Start with a few strokes every day, and reward with treats as necessary to show the pup that brushing is a good thing.

> **Did you know...** that most Bernedoodles will shed as their adult coat comes in? Expect to brush your puppy more often at this point to prevent the undercoat from matting, and consider a close clip to get a fresh start.

Many people make daily grooming a ritual. For example, you could put aside a few minutes every evening to brush your puppy. Later, when it's an adult, you can follow up the dog's final walk with a good brushing. Some of my clients report that brushing their Bernedoodle while watching TV is a pleasant way to end the day for both of them.

And remember, brushing your dog is one of the simplest and most effective methods for bonding with him or her—and in that way, the downside becomes the upside again!

> **An owner says…** *When the fur is long, it has to be done daily, but it's a very relaxing task that I enjoy.*

Tools and Techniques

While most people use the common, garden variety slicker brush for regular brushing, some maintain that a comb is better for getting at the fine undercoat, where mats form. What everyone agrees on is that the best technique is to "line comb," or lift the fur section by section, and comb from the root. You can start with firm strokes against the lay of the fur and then comb each layer in the direction it grows. Make sure you get down to the skin to comb out the fine undercoat, which is where mats form. Pay particular attention to the areas that tend to mat, including the underarms.

GROOMING ESSENTIALS

Universal Slicker brush - large

Greyhound 7.5" Long Pin. Fine\Coarse

8.25 inch Straight Scissors

44 Tooth Thinning Scissors

Millers Forge Large Dog Nail Clipper

WAHL Arco SE Cordless Clipper - *silver*

WAHL 5 in 1 Slide On Stainless Steel Guide Combs

Double K Challengair 2000XL 2 Speed Dryer

An owner says… *A long toothed comb is the secret weapon. It can be purchased anywhere. You have to make sure you are able to get down to the skin. If you line brush with a comb, mats will never occur.*

You may want to spray the dog lightly with water mixed with a drop of conditioner, as it's easier on the fur. There are also products you can apply to a mat to make it easier to break up. Cornstarch is a cheap and handy aid to use on mats. Gradually tease the matted fur apart by gently pulling it sideways, until it is at a point where you can comb it out. If all else fails, cut the mat out with scissors, being careful not to cut the skin. Luckily, a Bernedoodle's coat tends to be shaggy and forgiving. It's unlikely that people will notice a missing bit of fur here and there.

An owner says… *For breaking up mats that won't take a chunk of fur out, leaving a ghastly hole, I use an envelope opener. It's much safer than the sharp edge of shears, as well as easily controlled by the user. There is nothing like a slicker brush used daily to keep the coat fresh, light and un-matted. I also use an eight-inch double-sided comb, wide toothed on one edge, narrow on the other.*

Owners recommend…

Les Poochs is one of the best powerhouse brushes on the market. Expensive but built to last… I use it every day and it looks as good as new.

I'm fond of a product called The Stuff. You can use it on wet or dry fur and it makes combing and brushing so much easier.

All this time you are investing regularly will likely come back to you in cash when you take your dog for professional grooming. Most groomers charge more to work on a heavily matted dog, and just end up shaving it anyway.

Unless your Bernedoodle is inclined to roll in nasty things, I suggest bathing your dog infrequently—perhaps every three months—to avoid stripping oils from the coat. Often mud can simply be brushed off after the dog dries. If you do need to get your dog into the tub more often, try a lukewarm rinse using only conditioner or natural oatmeal shampoo to freshen him up.

Did you know that… bathing your dog when it's matted will make the mats tighter and nearly impossible to remove? Always comb out your dog before a bath. To reduce the chance of creating more mats, shampoo and condition with downward strokes—don't churn the fur around.

Every so often, you'll need to trim the hair around your dog's eyes so that you can gaze at each other (Come on, we all do it!)

A Trip to the Doodle Beauty Salon

It's a good idea to take your Bernedoodle puppy to a professional groomer when it is around four months old, or after it is fully vaccinated, so that it will get used to the experience. On the first visit, the puppy should only get a bath, brush, ear cleaning, and nail trim. On the next visit, the pup can get "the works," including a clip.

In the meantime, you will want to get recommendations from people about a reliable groomer. People who own nicely groomed Goldendoodles or Bernedoodles are a good place to start.

With daily care, you may be able to stretch out your time between clips to four months, but most people will need to go more frequently. Despite our best intentions, it is difficult to keep up with the daily maintenance. Sometimes, you just have to surrender your dog to the experts.

Now, you may scoff at little at the word, "experts," because some professional groomers often have a little trouble mastering the look most doodle owners like. After all, groomers are trained to like a nice, neat cut, and the typical doodle owner prefers something shaggier. Add to this that very few groomers will have encountered a Bernedoodle at all. So have patience with your groomer, and come armed with the photos I've included here—"Before" and "After" photos of my one of my standard Bernedoodles, with a nice winter and summer cut.

Deanna Ross is one of the groomers I use, and she kindly provided the instructions that follow so that you can provide them to your own groomer, or, if you're adventurous, tackle the job yourself.

Every breed has a standard for grooming—most of us would recognize a Poodle, Wheaton or Schnauzer cut instantly. I propose this as the standard cut for Bernedoodles.

Winter (Long) Cut

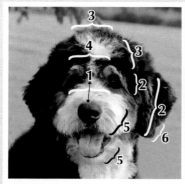
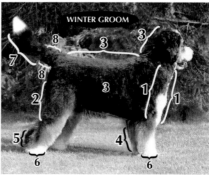

Brush your dog, and try to get out as many mats as possible before bathing.

Bath and dry, using forced air blow dryer. Use slicker brush and metal comb to get all the tangles out.

Use 40 blade on clippers to trim hair between pads, being careful not to trim up the sides of toes.

Body

1. Use a one-inch clipper comb and clip from chin to top of front legs on chest. Also on sides of neck, from under the ears to elbows.
2. Use one-inch clipper comb to clip on back of hind legs from base of tail to top of hocks.
3. Scissor body about three inches in length, blending body into clipped areas.
4. Scissor front legs in the shape of tubes from elbows to foot.
5. Scissor back legs in the shape of tubes, from top of hock to foot.
6. Pick up foot and turn over, so that you can comb hair over pads. Scissor hair so it is even with the pads. Then place the foot down and scissor around foot.

Tail

7. Scissor tail so that the hair is a little longer than the hair on the body.
8. Scissor blend hair on tail for about four inches from the dog's butt to longer area. The tail should look blended into the body.

Head

1. Use thinning scissors on top of muzzle from the nose to eyes. Cut hair short enough so that hair doesn't grow up in front of eyes.
2. Use half-inch clipper comb on cheeks, from edge of eyes to ears, under chin, and on ears.
3. Use three-quarter inch clipper comb on top of head from eyes to back of head, joining into cheeks.
4. Comb hair on top of head over eyes and scissor hair till eyes are showing.
5. Scissor under muzzle and side of muzzle to blend into the rest of the head.
6. Scissor edges of ears in the shape of the ear, about one-quarter inch from ear leather.

Summer Cut

Bath and dry, using forced air blow dryer. Use slicker brush and metal comb to get all the tangles out.

Use 40 blade on clippers to trim hair between pads, being careful not to trim up side of toes.

Body

1. Use a one-half inch clipper comb and clip from chin to top of front legs on chest. Also on sides of neck, from under the ears to elbows.
2. Use one-half inch clipper comb to clip on back of hind legs from base of tail to top of hocks.
3. Use seven-eighths inch clipper comb on body and down back of neck from back of head to the rest of the body.
4. Use a one-inch clipper comb on front legs, from elbows to foot.
5. Use a one-inch clipper comb on back legs, from top of hock to foot.
6. Pick up foot and turn over, so that you can comb hair over pads. Scissor hair so it is even with the pads. Then place the foot down and scissor around foot.

Tail

7. Scissor tail so that the hair is a little longer than the hair on the body.
8. Scissor blend hair on tail for about four inches from the dog's butt to longer area. The tail should look blended into the body.

Head

1. Use thinning scissors on top of muzzle from the nose to eyes. Take hair short enough so hair doesn't grow up in front of eyes.
2. Use half-inch clipper comb on the rest of the head, including muzzle and ears.
3. Comb hair on top of head over eyes and scissor hair till eyes are showing.
4. Scissor the muzzle so there are no long ends.
5. Scissor edges of ears in the shape of ear, about one-quarter inch from ear leather.

Make it easy for your groomer by taking in photos and explaining very carefully what you want. The SwissRidge Facebook page is an excellent resource for photos.

When you pick the dog up from the groomer, the cut may at first look a little short to your eye. Rest assured it will be perfect a couple of weeks later.

Even with these safeguards, at some point in your Bernedoodle's life, you may have a bad grooming experience. Most often this comes in the form of an extreme "poodling." Your Bernedoodle may have its muzzle shaved down, topped by a puff on the head and puffy ears. Worse, some people have come back to find their dog virtually unrecognizable because it had a very short shave from head to toe. It's quite a shock, and tears have been shed.

All I can say is that time heals all bad clips. This is an area of endless renewal. No cut is permanent.

The Debate about Ears

Most Bernedoodles have long, floppy ears that give them an endearing look, but can also make them prone to ear infections due to lack of airflow into the ear canal. Further, poodles have a tendency to have hairy ear canals, a trait that is often passed onto the Bernedoodle. I suggest having your groomer trim the hair under the ears short to increase airflow.

For regular maintenance, you can use cotton gauze soaked in a solution of 40 per cent vinegar and 60 per cent water to wipe out the ears. Never use cotton swabs in your dog's ear.

Veterinarians seem to be evenly split on the issue of plucking hair from the ear canal. Some think it prevents waxy buildup and ear infections; others think it can cause inflammation. I come down on the side of plucking. If you pull a bit at time, it causes very little discomfort to the dog. Start when your pup is young, and do a little once a week, using your fingers, a haemostat or tweezers. Clean the ear after plucking to prevent infection. This photo shows the area to pluck:

If your vet strongly disapproves, simply keep the ears very clean and monitor for ear infections. The first sign of trouble is often a yeasty smell, and then the dog will start shaking his head. Bernedoodles that swim regularly, and those with allergies, will be more prone to infections. Use an ear cleaning solution frequently, and a drying agent if the dog has been swimming.

When Things Start to Click

During your initial puppy wellness visit, your veterinarian should show you how to trim your puppy's nails and clean his teeth.

You can start trimming the tips of your pup's nails at a young age. Start by doing just one nail per day, and reward with a treat. In adulthood, you will likely need to make sure nails are trimmed every few weeks, depending on how much time the dog spends walking on asphalt and wearing them down.

If your dog has lighter-colored nails, you will be able to see the quick inside and easily avoid it when trimming. With darker nails, look in the underside to try to discern where the quick ends by looking for a hollow space at the end of the nail. If in doubt, ask for a lesson from your vet or a veterinary technician. Your groomer will likely have good advice as well.

You can also use a cordless dremel to sand the nail, if you are nervous about using clippers. It's a good idea to get the pup used to the dremel early. Start by showing him the object. Massage his face, body, tail and feet with it while giving him a treat. This way the dremel will have positive associations. Progress to turning the dremel on to get the pup used to the sound. Then you can apply the dremel to one nail for a second, and reward with a treat. When the dog accepts the dremel, you can use it for one or two seconds on each nail weekly.

It's All in the Smile

It's important to get your puppy used to having his teeth cleaned early to prevent tartar build up. As with humans, gum disease can cause systemic problems, such as kidney or heart damage. It can also lead to very costly veterinary dental care.

Use a puppy finger tooth brush and puppy toothpaste every day. When your pup reaches six months, you can switch to a regular toothbrush. *Never use toothpaste intended for humans.*

Aerobic oxygen will also help to keep your dog's mouth clean. You can find this at the health food store, and mix 25 drops into 25 millilitres of water. Spray it into the back of your dog's mouth to keep plaque from forming. It will keep its breath fresh, too.

Bringing Up the Rear

Finally, as part of your general routine, clip the fur around your dog's anus, using round-tipped scissors.

If you notice that your dog is sitting and scooting across the floor or grass, he may have impacted anal glands. Normally these glands are expressed with regular bowel movements, but small poops, or a bout of the runs, may result in impaction. Adding one tablespoon of canned pumpkin or psyllium will often firm a loose stool.

Most groomers will express the anal glands as part of regular grooming. A vet or vet technician may do a more thorough job, and can show you how to do it yourself, if you have the stomach for this stinky task.

I never claimed that owning a Bernedoodle would be all fun and games!

But I did promise that your hard work would pay steep dividends, and I stand by that.

Chapter 13

The Natural Dog

No one has a deeper appreciation for veterinary services than a breeder who owns a few dozen dogs. I'm fortunate to have a wonderful team of vets that I trust with my dogs' lives. That said, I rarely need to visit the vet for anything more than health testing.

My dogs are rotated between indoor and outdoor kennels, and I believe that living with other dogs in the fresh air keeps them healthy and hearty. I try not to baby them, and only give medication if it is absolutely needed. My approach seems to be working, as one of my first breeding dogs, a golden retriever named Ginger, is nearly 16. While she's slowing down, she still acts like a puppy sometimes.

I'm mindful of the fact that my situation is different from that of the average dog owner's. I live on a rural property with a large population of dogs. They are not exposed regularly to new dogs or common diseases, but if they did encounter an illness, it could spread like wildfire. Further, I need to be wary of exposing breeding dogs to medications that might harm them or their puppies. It's a fine balance that I discuss with my vets, and you will need to do the same in considering your circumstances.

I worry that people sometimes turn too quickly to pharmaceutical solutions when a natural approach may work just as well, and be better for a dog. These days, many vets are open to holistic solutions.

So, while I always encourage people to seek an expert's advice about any concern with their dogs, I present in this chapter some food for thought about natural options you might use with your dog, if the situation is not a veterinary 911.

(Please note that the suggestions below are just that—suggestions. While I've tried many of these approaches myself, or learned about them from my clients, they might not be right for every dog and could even cause harm if used inappropriately. I encourage you to do some research and check with your vet if you have questions.)

Nutritional Booster

The best defense is a strong offense, so I suggest keeping your dog in top shape by providing a high quality food, along with the following supplements—all of which I feed to my pack.

- Omega 3 and 6 oils – These fats are called essential fatty acids and they may be included in your dog's normal diet. They are particularly beneficial for a dog's skin and coat.
- Coconut oil – Unrefined coconut oil is thought to reduce risk of cancer, improve digestion, prevent or treat yeast and fungal infections, relieve arthritis and support healthy skin and coat. Applied topically, coconut oil can disinfect cuts, improve skin and coat condition, and clear up rashes.
- Tumeric – Used as a supplement, turmeric's anti-inflammatory and antibacterial properties show promise in the prevention and treatment of cancer. Turmeric can also help reduce arthritis inflammation and pain in pets.
- Norwegian Kelp – Kelp is considered to be a rich source of natural minerals, vitamins and amino acids. In dogs, it can reduce stress and improve digestion, enhance skin and coat condition, improve dry skin, and help with allergies.
- Coenzyme Q10 (CoQ10) – This essential coenzyme supports cells with the highest turnover rate, such as heart cells, mouth tissue cells, intestinal mucosal cells and immune system cells. In pets, it contributes to healthy circulation, promotes optimal immune function and supports cardiovascular health.
- Probiotics – Adding a probiotic to your dog's diet should improve digestion and immune function. Probiotics are particularly helpful if your dog has had antibiotic treatment, changed to a new food, has a food allergy, inflammatory bowel disease, or is a senior or a puppy. You can give your dog a probiotic such as FortiFlora, or a

dog-specific supplement. Plain yogurt and kefir are also good sources.

- Nuvet supplements, as mentioned earlier.

I've deliberately avoided providing dosage amounts to encourage you to do your own research, and consult with your vet. I do recommend starting with a small amount of any supplement and increasing as tolerated.

You may want to check out the following resources on holistic approaches:

- *The Royal Treatment* by Dr. Barbara Royal
- *Real Food for Healthy Dogs and Cats* by Dr. Karen Becker (Dr. Becker's website, is also a great resource)
- www.WholeDogJournal.com
- www.earthanimal.com

Parasite Patrol – Part 1

Dogs can pick up fleas and ticks anywhere. It's important to have a plan for parasites, but that plan doesn't necessarily mean a pharmaceutical solution, about which there is some controversy.

Believe it or not, I have never had fleas at my kennel, despite my strict avoidance of the typically prescribed medications. My only strategy is simple: I quarantine any new dog that arrives at the kennel, keeping it away from my other dogs for two weeks. I also sprinkle a new dog's fur with animal grade Diatomaceous earth as a precautionary measure. Once I'm sure it is flea and disease free, the new dog can join the pack.

Diatomaceous earth, or "D-earth," is a natural product made from tiny fossilized skeletal remains of unicellular plants called diatoms. It has the appearance of talcum powder, but for insects, it's a lethal dust that cuts their protective outer covering. Animal grade D-earth (not pool grade!) kills insects, but is harmless to humans and pets. You can sprinkle it around the house or rub on your pet to get rid of fleas.

People who take their dogs to public dog parks face more challenges than I do in this regard. But if you are reluctant to give flea medications to your dog, there are a number of holistic repellants you can try, in addition to D-earth.

- Apple cider vinegar not only helps strengthen the immune system, it makes a dog less tasty to fleas. Try a teaspoon daily in your dog's drinking water. You can also dilute cider vinegar 50:50 with water, pour into a spray bottle and apply it directly to skin.
- Rosemary is another natural flea repellant. Steep two cups of fresh rosemary in boiling water for 30 minutes. Strain the liquid, discard the leaves and add to a gallon of warm water, depending on the size of your dog. While the fluid is still warm, pour over the dog until it is soaked. Allow the dog to dry naturally.
- Lavender Essential Oil – Apply a few drops of lavender oil to the base of the tail and the neck of your freshly bathed dog.
- Citrus Spray – Cut a lemon, lime, orange or grapefruit into quarters, cover with boiling water and let steep overnight. In the morning, pour the solution into a spray bottle and apply it to the dog, especially behind the ears and around the head (avoid the eyes!), around the base of the tail, and under the legs.
- Nematode worms, available at garden shops and pet stores, like to eat flea larvae. They can help to keep the outdoor flea population controlled.
- Water – A good douse in the tub can flush fleas away. A gentle shampoo, or natural liquid dish detergent, can help as well.

If you do end up with a flea problem, sprinkle D-earth around the house, launder your pet's bedding frequently, and vacuum thoroughly, disposing of the vacuum cleaner bag. Repeat in two weeks, in case you missed any flea eggs.

Ticked Off

Ticks deserve a special mention, because they are common in some areas and carry disease. I have only seen two ticks on my dogs in all my years of breeding, but we continue to check for them every day.

The first line of attack is your immediate environment. Get rid of tick-friendly foliage and long, damp grass. Keep your yard mowed and trimmed, and remove dead and overgrown vegetation. Ticks dislike dry heat, so let the sun into as many parts of your yard as possible.

Fence your yard to prevent animals such as deer or coyotes from passing through and leaving ticks and fleas behind.

Spray the yard and the dog with a natural tick repellent, such as the citrus spray noted above. For good measure, apply rose geranium oil to your dog's collar.

If you live in an area where ticks are common and your dog spends a lot of time in the woods or fields, you can also try making some leg warmers or trousers for your dog out of old socks or a child's sweater—anything to impede the ticks from latching.

Check your dog regularly for ticks. If you find one, use tweezers or a specially designed tool to remove the entire tick. Follow these steps:

- Put on latex or rubber gloves to avoid direct contact with the tick.
- Enlist someone to help immobilize your dog during the extraction.
- Apply rubbing alcohol to the bite area, before using a pair of tweezers to grasp the tick as close to the dog's skin as possible. Pull straight upwards with steady, even pressure. Don't twist the tick, as it may leave mouth-parts behind, or cause the tick to regurgitate infective fluids. Make sure all the mouth parts are out.
- Place the tick in a jar with rubbing alcohol.
- Disinfect the bite site, and sterilize your tweezers with alcohol.
- Monitor the bite site for any signs of infection. If the area becomes inflamed, take your dog—along with the dead tick—to your vet for evaluation. The vet will send the tick away to test it for Lyme disease.

Parasite Patrol – Part Two

Worms are not a popular topic of conversation, but they are a reality in a dog's life.

While I have been very lucky with fleas and ticks, I do have to take a proactive stance with parasites such as worms. With a large group of dogs running around my yard, eating grass and swimming in a pond, worms are unavoidable. We do everything in our power to prevent them, and keep them from spreading, including power washing pens daily and bathing dogs on a regular basis.

Still, many dogs have larvae in their tissue, which can emerge in times of stress, including during pregnancy. The larvae can migrate through the placenta and infect the pups. After birth, pups can be infected through the mother's milk.

De-worming medications are my only viable option. Even then, as moms clean up after their pups, they can re-infect themselves. It's an ongoing challenge and for the most part, I am successful. However, a few pups may leave my kennel with parasites. That's why I suggest taking a stool sample to the initial vet visit. Left unchecked, parasites can not only make the puppy sick, but other pets and even people.

If you do need to treat your dog for worms, be sure to bath it every day during the treatment. The larvae that are shed by the dog can stick to the coat, and the dog may re-ingest them by licking. Also be vigilant about picking up your dog's feces to make sure it does not re-infect itself or infect other dogs.

Holistic approaches may help in your situation. Try tinctures of black walnut hull or doses of wormwood, which are used against intestinal worms such as hookworms and tapeworms.

Adding a tiny amount of ground cloves to your pet's diet may help to ward off parasites.

Some pet owners report success in using chewing tobacco as a natural agent to kill parasites quickly.

The Shots

Recently there has been criticism about routine dog vaccines, in regards to their effectiveness and potential side effects. While I stay informed about research suggesting we are over-vaccinating our pets, I support immunizing dogs.

In my view, it's essential that dogs be protected from common diseases like rabies and parvo. Parvo is still very common, and I've known other breeders to lose multiple dogs and litters to the disease.

However, while the initial rounds of puppy shots are crucial, it may be possible to avoid vaccinating your dog annually once it reaches adulthood. I recommend asking your vet to run a titer that measures your dog's antibodies to certain antigens in the bloodstream. A positive titer test result may mean your dog has sufficient resistance to disease and you can skip the vaccine.

> **An owner says...** *Thought I'd let you know that we got Morgan's titer back for parvo and he is absolutely good for the antibodies—no vaccination required. Interesting that it's over three years since he's had any vaccines and he's still good. That's awesome, but also makes it clear that the annual vaccine thing is definitely an overkill and with the potential to do way more harm than good.*

Allergies

While none of my dogs have allergies—and would be retired from breeding if they did—I know that an increasing number of dogs do. In fact, it has become the biggest health issue I've seen in Bernedoodles and Goldendoodles. There are many theories on the increasing incidence of allergies, which I won't speculate on here, other than to say that our environment and toxins may be contributing.

Dogs can react to airborne allergens, insect bites, food or anything that comes into contact with the skin. Symptoms of allergies include rashes, itchy and watery eyes, sneezing, and ear infections.

If you suspect food is the cause, switch to one that is grain free and has a single protein (e.g., fish and sweet potato). Avoid treats and chew bones until you've determined the source of the problem.

Many of the food supplements noted above, especially fish oils, can be helpful in alleviating the inflammation associated with allergies. Digestive enzymes can also reduce inflammation, and bolster beneficial bacteria. (Note: It is important to not supplement with digestive enzymes if the dog's intestinal flora are out of balance). Finally, Ester C is thought to be helpful in reducing allergic reactions.

Some other strategies:

- Bathe your dog with oatmeal shampoo once a week to reduce allergens on the coat (frequent baths are fine if you are trying to keep allergies at bay).
- Wipe your dog's feet after going outside for a walk.
- Be vigilant about flea protection.
- Use hypoallergenic products to launder the dog's bedding; vacuum and dust frequently.
- Avoid air fresheners and chemical cleaning products.

If your dog is itchy, chamomile tea can help. Cool and pour it into a spray bottle. Apply directly to irritated skin.

Another great natural treatment is vitamin E oil, which you can apply to itchy skin.

Finally, there's the old standby, oatmeal. Add water to finely ground oatmeal and rub the paste onto itchy areas. Leave on for 10 minutes and rinse with warm water.

If your dog's allergies are severe enough, your vet may prescribe a medication like Benadryl or steroids. But do try the holistic approaches before turning to medications that may have side effects.

Keeping it Clean

I recommend using organic natural shampoos on your dog and avoiding any products that contain harsh ingredients such as Ammonium Chloride, Propylene Glycol, Methylisothiazoline, Sodium Lauryl Sulfate and the related chemical Sodium Laureth Sulfate, Parabens. Phthalates, Formaldehyde, Propylene Glycol, Diethanolamine Polyethylene Glycol, and Salicylic Acid. Labels such as "Strong Fragrance" or "Parfum" are often a catch-all for many different chemicals.

There are many reports of adverse reactions to these chemicals. I would discourage you from using them on your dog—or yourself!

Aches and Pains

If your dog begins limping, it may have strained a ligament in play. It's time to try the world famous granny remedy of an Epsom salt soak. Add a half cup of Epsom salt to a warm bath and let your dog soak for five minutes, twice daily. If your dog won't cooperate, try soaking a washcloth in Epsom salts and warm water and applying it to the affected area.

If your dog limps or is in pain, I suggest limiting its activity and taking it to the vet for examination as soon as possible. Tearing a ligament can be extremely painful for a pup.

Some medium or large breed dogs can get an inflammatory condition called Panosteitis, which affects the long bones of young, rapidly-growing pups. Your vet may give you a pain reliever to help, but eventually your dog will outgrow the condition.

Bring it Up

Many Bernedoodles will devour whatever they can get their jaws around. In some instances, you can reverse the situation quickly, but call your vet to be sure. To induce vomiting, give the dog one teaspoon of hydrogen peroxide for every 10 pounds of body weight. You can use an eyedropper, syringe or turkey baster aimed to the back of your dog's throat. This method will take up to 20 minutes to take effect. Repeat once if needed.

If in doubt, consult with the veterinary experts. I do!

Chapter 14

I receive hundreds of e-mails every week. There are common questions that surface time and again, so I thought I'd include some of them here.

What are the main differences between standard, mini and tiny Bernedoodles, and which one would be right for me?

Usually the smaller the dog the more energetic it is. So standards are the most laid back, mini-Bernedoodles are more active, and tiny Bernedoodles are the most active.

However, in saying this, I don't see a huge difference in energy among any of them, because I breed for a calm, laid back temperament regardless of size.

When you are looking for a breeder, you will need to make sure he or she is consciously breeding calm good-tempered dogs, because—I've said it before, and it bears repeating—hyper parents produce hyper puppies and aggressive parents produce aggressive pups.

Many miniature and toy Poodles are hyperactive and yappy, and their pups would be hard to control. I've had to work hard to find calm, good-tempered Poodles in all sizes to ensure that my Bernedoodles get the Poodle intelligence and playfulness, but not excessive energy. I want my dogs to be active enough to join their families on all kinds of activities, but calm enough to slow down when required.

Standards Bernedoodles are large, regal, and stunning. They have an amazing presence, and are imposing enough to serve as protectors. Yet they tend to be soft-hearted lapdogs.

Medium Bernedoodles are the most popular, because of their moderate size. They suit just about any situation, and many people think they are easier to handle than a Standard.

Tiny Bernedoodles are perfect for those who live in small spaces, but still want "big dog" spirit. Most tiny Bernedoodles don't realize they're pint-sized and they have tons of confidence.

Although large breed dogs are usually lazier than small breed dogs, I think small dogs don't get enough respect. If bred correctly, they have just as much potential as a larger dog to be well-trained. In fact, I think people have lower expectations for their small dogs. They do less training and impose fewer boundaries. For example, people let their small dogs on the furniture or beds more than large dogs. I always tell people who buy mini or tiny Bernedoodles to treat them exactly as they would a dog that would grow up to be 80 pounds. This way you will have a well behaved small dog when they mature.

I will acknowledge a notable difference in relation to size, however. The smaller the dog, the lower the cost of maintenance—from food, to grooming, to vet bills.

How will I know if my Bernedoodle's colors will change?

When a pup is eight weeks of age, its undercoat will usually indicate its adult coloring. If you see silver at the base of the coat, your Bernedoodle's coat will change substantially as it matures. However, some Bernedoodles may change color even later, turning grey or white before they reach the age of two years.

Some breeders won't know if colors will change. In the early stages of breeding Bernedoodles, I did not know, either. I have now bred enough litters to be pretty certain of the likelihood of a Bernedoodle's coat colors remaining fixed.

If coat color is really important to you, make sure you discuss this with your breeder. I would suggest asking to see photos of pups a particular pairing has produced in the past. The safest bet is an experienced breeder that has a good reputation. A breeder should be keeping in touch with clients to keep tabs on how puppies are turning out.

How can I estimate how big my Bernedoodle will become?

I can provide a range of weights for a litter, and can usually give a ballpark based on the size of the puppy at eight weeks, relative to its littermates. However, some pups surprise me.

The following formula may give you an idea of how much your pup of 22 weeks will weigh in adulthood:

Current weight in pounds divided by age (in weeks) multiplied by 52.

For example, take a mini Bernedoodle that is 13 pounds at 22 weeks.

13 divided by 22 = .5909 pounds multiplied by 52 = 30.72 lbs

A medium-sized puppy's growth will be slowing at 22 weeks, while large puppies are still growing fast. Also, males are usually larger than females.

How does a miniature Poodle male mate with a female Bernese Mountain Dog?

When a male dog is substantially smaller than a female, the pregnancy is almost always the result of artificial insemination.

How do I deal with a picky eater who often skips meals?

This is probably the most common question I receive from my clients.

It's very common for Bernedoodles (or Goldendoodles, for that matter) to be picky, because Poodles are notoriously selective eaters. Unlike Labrador Retrievers, which will inhale any food that comes their way, Poodles tend to eat only exactly what they need, when they need it. This is completely normal.

Like their Poodle ancestors, many Bernedoodles will eat only when they need food, not simply because food is available. Puppies may eat ravenously when they are having a growth spurt, and taper off in between. Also, dogs will lose their appetite in very warm weather. While picky eating is worrisome for owners, especially when the dog is young, keep in mind that it is far healthier for a dog to be slim.

I always reassure clients that their picky eater is perfectly fine, unless you also see the following: lethargy, vomiting, loose stools, a high temperature, or weight loss. Over time, you will discover what is normal for your dog, and recognize when things are off, and you need to see a vet.

It's not a good idea to start enhancing a dog's regular food with special treats, because he may come to expect it, and spurn his kibble. I've seen a lot of dogs that aren't hungry for their kibble suddenly develop an appetite when steak is within reach. Dogs will hold out for better if they think they can get it. Don't force the issue. Your Bernedoodle will eat when it's hungry.

How do you feel about free-feeding?

I recommend feeding young puppies three times a day, and cutting that to twice a day when the dog is older. Having a set time for meals and water will help tremendously with housebreaking, because you can figure out the pup's elimination pattern and work with it. If you free-feed, it is much harder to predict when a pup needs to go out. Further, free-feeding can lead to obesity in pets. So stick to a schedule—you'll be happy you did! In the long term, free-feeding can lead to obesity in pets.

What's the best way to socialize a puppy before it's had all its vaccines?

Your first week is mainly about bonding with your puppy quietly at home. After that, you can start inviting people over to meet the pup, making sure they leave their shoes at the door and wash their hands. Introduce the pup to children, if there are none in your household, but keep a close eye on them. To start socializing your pup with other dogs, the perfect solution is play-dates at your home with healthy, vaccinated dogs. You can also introduce your puppy to all sorts of things in the house that it will later encounter in the real world, such as different noises, umbrellas, or skateboards.

How do I deal with my dog's anxiety in the car?

Most pups get car sick, and most grow out of it.

Try to keep car rides positive by making it an adventure. Take the pup on short trips that end somewhere fun. For example, drive over to visit a friend that has a fun doggy playmate. That way the dog develops positive associations with the car. Lengthen the rides gradually to increase tolerance.

If car sickness continues, here are some other suggestions:

- Avoid meals before car rides.
- Keep the window open for fresh air.

- Make sure the dog is facing forward in the front seat (bearing in mind the risk of an airbag deploying).
- Try natural ginger or mint remedies for dogs.
- As a last resort, speak to your veterinarian about medications.

My dog is very nervous in thunder storms. What can I do?

Valerian root, found in health food stores, can have a calming effect on dogs. Discuss the appropriate amount with your vet.

The "Thundershirt" apparently works wonders for dog anxiety.

My dog is five years old and is really slowing down. Should I be worried?

As dogs age, they do slow down. This is normal. I recommend switching to a food for senior dogs at the age of eight, and start giving the dog a joint supplement.

What are some fun activities to do with my Bernedoodle?

For puppies that are still growing, I suggest fetch, swimming, and basic obedience, which is fun for the dog because they love learning.

When a dog is older, depending on the dog's personality, you can try therapy dog training, dock jumping, tracking, hiking, obedience trials, swimming, or agility.

I am a big fan of agility training, as it's a fun way to reinforce obedience. It's best not to start until the dog has fully matured, however—at least a year for miniature Bernedoodles, and 18 months for standards. The younger they are, the more careful you should be to keep the course easy—no high jumps, and no more than once a week.

I am also thrilled that Bernedoodles are turning out to be great therapy dogs, whether it's formal training, or just within the family.

An Owner Says… My son has Tourette's Syndrome and [our Bernedoodle's] sensitivity and empathetic traits have shone through during difficult times. When my son is having his tutoring session, the dog always sits right on his lap, almost as though she knows he needs her to be there. My son has commented on how she makes him feel calm. And I have to say, since bringing the puppy home, he has not had one Tourette's outburst (Before, this could be a weekly or bi-weekly occurrence).

My Bernedoodle does not like the water. How can I encourage her to swim?

If she's still a puppy, get a children's pool in your back yard and introduce her to water in a familiar environment. Expose her to other dogs that are swimming and having fun, and try throwing sticks in the water. Get into the water yourself and call her to join you. Above all, make the water seem like the most fun place to be.

How can I prevent snow from caking on my Bernedoodle's coat?

If moving to Florida is not an option, I recommend keeping the dog's coat shorter to limit snow accumulation. You can also apply a "show sheen" product, meant to give horses a shiny coat, before heading into a blizzard. Spray it on your dog where snowballs usually accumulate. (Do this outside, as it makes the floor slippery!)

Wintery weather can also be very hard on a dog's paws. I suggest booties to protect paws from salt and sharp ice.

I have a Bernedoodle and want to get a second dog. What breed do you recommend?

Bernedoodles are social, easygoing dogs, so any combination should work. However, I hear all the time that doodles gravitate towards one another in parks, perhaps because of their bouncy, fun-loving nature. I think two Bernedoodles, or a Bernedoodle and Goldendoodle are ideal pairings. But, of course, I am a little biased.

How important are spaying and neutering?

I believe in spaying and neutering so strongly that it is part of my contract. Females that aren't spayed can develop Pyometrium, and are also more prone to certain types of cancer. Further, unaltered females will bleed and be temperamental while in season.

Unneutered males can become territorial and aggressive, and are more prone to testicular cancer.

What do you like best about being a dog breeder?

That's easy! I absolutely love the joy my puppies bring. So many people have told me that their dog has changed their life for the better. Some have said the dog brought their family closer together or brought new purpose to their lives. I think a dog is man's best therapist.

This makes me forget the few downsides to this job, including the long hours, many sleepless nights and the fact that there is rarely a silent moment at my house.

What do you like least?

That is also easy: losing a puppy or a dog. In all the years of breeding, I haven't managed to steel myself against that. When it happens, I feel like my heart is being ripped out of my chest. If a puppy is stillborn, it depresses me. And every day a puppy or dog lives with me just intensifies a loss when it comes.

On the flipside, there are situations where I have managed to save puppies that nature didn't intend to survive. There have been many runts I've nurtured back to health through bottle feeding, plasma, and lots of love and special care. I remember every one of those runts, and delight in how well they are doing with their new owners. I know that if it weren't for all my hard work they wouldn't be here today.

If you had to choose one favorite trait about Bernedoodles, what would it be?

Okay, that's a tough one, because I love nearly everything about them! I guess if I had to pick one thing, it's that they are characters. They have such personality. I'll let some of my clients speak for me, here:

Our mini Bernedoodle is a pup full of life. She is very vocal (likes to talk) and is extremely curious. If she was a child, she would probably spend her day doing puzzles and figuring out brain teasers, and most likely setting up practical jokes around the house to trap us all in. She can also be found sitting on the window sill watching the world go by, absorbing everything she sees. Sula can also entertain herself by playing catch and throwing her own toys in the air and catching them on their down fall. Raglan, our standard, knows how to have fun, but is a bit more serious. He is very in tune with all the family members, and will not go to bed until all his "kids" are home.

Alfie's temperament is best described as a puppy-version of Dennis the Menace. I mean this in the best way possible. To the casual outsider or visitor, he may seem energetic and excitable. This is because he absolutely loves people (especially kids) and finds it difficult to contain his enthusiasm for new and old friends... He is very curious and loves exploring... He is mischievous: the geese in the park remember him and chase us down in revenge for his startle tactics.

If she wants to show a mischievous side she gets stuffed animals from the kids' rooms (doesn't chew them up) and lines them up by the front door awaiting my arrival.

Sadie loves to dance. I swear one day she is just going to decide she wants to walk on two legs instead of four. She is so short and stubby I feel she jumps up in order to feel more in the action. She hops, jumps and dances all on her two hind legs. It is the funniest thing to watch... she loves people so much she has to get as close to them as possible.

He is a funny guy with a few quirks. He does not like being laughed at... He actually gets upset and might bark or go sulk ever so briefly. He is quite talkative and will vocalize his doggy opinions readily.

Cassie is funny, beautiful, loving and VERY smart... She is sooo agile. She amazes us. She does get into trouble lots. She can get into places that other dogs can't and so we have to hide everything. She's sweet, mischievous playful and independent.

...Happy, happy and oh ya, happy

Did you make up that last question as an excuse for more testimonials?

Heh heh. Was it that obvious? But since you brought it up, here's another one.

She has been a dream! Sure, we have a few items to work through but she has been a dream dog. She is easy to train, SO loving, and wants to be such a part of our family.

I mean seriously, hearing things like that all the time, who wouldn't want my job?

Do you have a favorite dog?

I love all dogs, but try very hard not to develop favorites. I can't make objective decisions about my breeding program if I've bonded too closely with a dog. So I do my best to treat them all the same, and keep my guard up at all times.

That's why it came as a huge surprise to me recently when I fell for an unlikely suspect: a Miniature Poodle puppy named Dizzy. Miniature Poodles are not really my type. I generally prefer a bigger, more rugged dog; I love "lots" of dog. But somehow little Dizzy ambushed me with his sweet personality and utter devotion, and weaseled his way into my heart. A complete charmer, he dances on his hind legs like a circus dog, and wins over everyone he meets. No matter where Dizzy is in the house, if we summon him with kissing sounds, he comes running as fast as he can. He'll whine and roll on his back until he gets cuddled and showered with kisses. Needless to say, this behavior has seen a lot of positive reinforcement!

Dizzy is an exceptional dog. If he passes his health clearances, he will produce some very sweet puppies. And if he doesn't, well, this dog isn't going anywhere. He's not just "one of my dogs"—he truly is *my* dog.

I only confess this here, because it proves everything I said earlier about temperament being absolutely the most important thing when selecting a dog. A mini Poodle may not be my "dream dog," but Dizzy's temperament has made him absolutely perfect in my eyes. I wouldn't trade my precious pup for anything.

It's a wonderful thing if you can get the "whole package," but in the end, what really counts is personality. So instead of holding out for a stunning tri-colored Bernedoodle, you may want to "settle" for one with the best personality for you and your family. It will be the start of a long and beautiful relationship.

Afterword

Breeding beautiful, tri-color Bernedoodles was a truly a watershed moment in my career. Although I'd developed a solid strategy for breeding healthy dogs with a great temperament, producing Bernedoodles that looked just like my beloved Bernese Mountain Dogs was unexpectedly challenging.

I enjoyed every minute of figuring it out. In fact, the process made me realize that I love breeding for more than the obvious reasons (puppies and happy clients!). I'm fascinated by genetic puzzles. The best part about being an intrepid breeder-adventurer is that every experiment has a happy ending, whether or not it leads exactly where I expect. The most important thing is that all of my dogs go to great homes.

I am very satisfied with the Bernedoodles I am producing. While I will continue to try new pairings, I think I've pretty much reached my destination on this breed.

That means I am ready to start planning my next great breeding adventure. I have a vision in mind of the ultimate SwissRidge doodle: a low- to non-shedding wavy/fleece coat, a variety of colors and markings, and great proportions, all in a mid-sized package. It goes without saying that this dog will possess all the traits my clients have come to expect of a SwissRidge dog. It will be intelligent, trainable, calm, loyal, playful, fun, gentle and great with kids—the ultimate companion dog. And of course it will also be healthy, with many generations of genetically cleared ancestors behind it.

This vision may take a few years to achieve, because there are no shortcuts in conscientious professional breeding. To create something new, I need to start with plenty of healthy, even-tempered parents and work incrementally toward my goal.

I've already taken the first step of this journey with my April 2013 cross between a Bernedoodle and a Goldendoodle, a hybrid my clients named the "Golden Mountain Doodle." To my knowledge, this litter of nine was the first of its kind and I'm excited to see how they turn out. They are gorgeous, healthy pups, and if positive reviews continue to roll in, there may be more such litters along the way.

Please visit my website periodically for updates on the new hybrid-in-the-making. I haven't been so excited about a project since… well, since I started breeding Bernedoodles!

Also in development is a new custom-designed facility for SwissRidge Kennels that exceeds industry standards. This facility will not only house my dogs, but also provide space for boarding and spa services, and an expanded training program. I expect to break ground in 2014.

It's an exciting time at SwissRidge Kennels. And if I could change one thing about my life as a breeder… I wouldn't.

Author's note:

> *Word-of-mouth is incredibly important for both breeders and authors to succeed. If you enjoyed this book, please consider leaving a review where you purchased it. Even a line or two would help, and would be very much appreciated.*

If you would like to hear about the latest news at SwissRidge Kennels, please sign up for my newsletter on the homepage at Swissridgekennels.com. Your address will never be shared.

Acknowledgements

I want to express my deepest appreciation to my parents, Chris Rupke and Patricia Moor. I don't think they believed I could make a career out of dog breeding, yet they supported me anyway—encouraging me to follow my dreams and making me believe that hard work could accomplish wonders. It has! By looking after my dogs for me while I was in college, my dad made it possible for me to keep my business alive. My mom continues to be a huge help to this day. Without my parents' support, I may not have found my way to the best job in the world.

Without Lucas Mucha, I would not enjoy this job nearly as much. As my long-time boyfriend and best friend, Lucas is there for me, day in and day out. Dog breeding is very demanding business, but Lucas is always willing to support my next great idea—even when it means upheaval for him. I respect and admire Lucas' talent for training, and I've learned so much from him. I'm constantly amazed at my good luck in finding someone who fits so perfectly into my life.

Like most breeders, I have a sincere appreciation for veterinary services, and I have an amazing group behind me: the staff at Beaverton Crossroads Veterinary Services.

Rick Doner has been my role model since I was just a little girl with a big love of animals. Volunteering for him inspired me to dedicate my life to raising dogs. Moreover, Rick's high standards have shaped my own practices at SwissRidge Kennels. I aspire to do my very best by my dogs, and Rick was the first to show me how.

Les Sadoch has become a huge part of caring for my canine family. He's basically available 24/7, and that gives me such peace of mind. I count on Les to help me through tough choices, and I'm always learning from him. Lately, he's given me excellent advice about building my new kennel. He is not only my vet but a dear friend.

Aimee Gilbert is one of the nicest and most accommodating vets I've met. I'm always glad to see her, along with the other wonderful staff at Beaverton Crossroads, including Carrie, Ruth, Megan, Rea, Kelly, Dayna and Jill, Martina, Sharon, and Elaine. You are truly the best.

All of my dogs land in good homes, and some of those homes yield wonderful friends. Some of those friends have been a big help with this book and beyond.

First, there's Sandy Rideout, who adopted Riggs—possibly the cutest puppy I've ever produced (okay, she made me say that). Without Sandy, this book would still be in my very long "to do" list. A dog novice until recently, Sandy has gone above and beyond in getting to know me, my business, and my clients. I can't thank her enough for the time she has put into this book and helping me capture exactly what I wanted to say. I've been impressed with the way she handled this project and the research involved. I'm so glad our paths crossed.

Next is Karley Gittens, owner of Zolo, and a Bernedoodle yet to be born. Karley is a skilled graphic designer who is ready at the drop of a hat to take an ordinary image and make it exceptional. She's helped me with many projects, from the doodle romp to my website, and now this book. You can find Karley at www.gittencreative.com

Then there's Doreen Alessi-Holmes, owner of Gizmo and Marley, and Cathy Spata Martini, owner of Paisley. The SwissRidge Facebook page is a better place to hang out because of their wisdom, kindness and good humor. I'm so pleased they agreed to review this book in advance and provide their valuable input.

I would also like to thank Meg, a very special client and friend, who's given three of my dogs an amazing home, and given me experiences I will never forget. Meg, you've brought me closer to achieving my dream and I thank you from the bottom of my heart for the kindness you have shown me. You are truly an inspiration. I love talking to you and watching your boys grow. Long may our friendship thrive.

Circling back home, I want to thank all SwissRidge staff, past and present, who have made my life much easier. Leeann MacKay deserves particular mention. Although she has only been working with me for a year, she's already a key member of the SwissRidge family. Quite simply, I don't know how I ran the business without her. Leann is a Godsend, and everyone needs someone like her in their lives. I look forward to expanding my business with her help.

Last, I want to thank each and every one of my many wonderful clients. Without you there would be no SwissRidge Kennels. As a breeder, finding good homes for my dogs is my top priority and I simply could not ask for better clients. My dogs become treasured members of great families. I know this because their owners usually keep in touch, and hearing how happy they are makes me push even harder to breed amazing dogs.

Now that my clients have gathered as a community on the SwissRidge Facebook page, I get to see photos and hear stories about their dogs every single day. It's like a truly great party, where you all share a common interest. The SwissRidge Doodle Romp provides an opportunity to meet in person—and raise money for a good cause.

Special thanks to the Bernedoodle owners who provided ideas, input and photos for this book. Hearing how much you are enjoying this breed made me love my work even more—and I didn't think that was possible.

About the Authors

Sherry Rupke grew up on a farm near Beaverton, Ontario, and began breeding dogs at age 15. Inspired by her volunteer work at Beaverton Crossroads Veterinary Services, Sherry became a certified Veterinary Technician in 2004. In establishing SwissRidge Kennels, Sherry set a goal of producing healthy, happy hybrids dogs that suit any family. Her breed lines continue to evolve, along with the stringent standards of her breeding program. The result is a widespread and growing community of satisfied clients. To meet them, search Facebook for "SwissRidge Kennels" and join the group. You can learn more about Sherry's Bernedoodles and Goldendoodles at www.bernedoodles.com and www.swissridgekennels.com

Sandy Rideout grew up a cat lover, and crossed over to the dog side when she adopted a mini Goldendoodle from Sherry in 2012. Sandy asked Sherry to find her the perfect writer's dog—one with an "off" switch. A year later, Riggins is turning out to be exactly as Sherry promised. As for the months in between, well, Sandy could have used a book like this. That is why she jumped at the chance to take a look "behind the curtain" at SwissRidge Kennels to see how Sherry works her magic, alongside trainer extraordinaire, Lucas Mucha. You can learn more about Sandy and her books at www.sandyrideout.com

Made in the USA
Columbia, SC
04 January 2020